THE UNANSWERED QUESTIONS ABOUT PRESIDENT KENNEDY'S ASSASSINATION

By SYLVAN FOX

AWARD BOOKS • NEW YORK

AWARD BOOKS
First Printing October, 1965
Second Printing November, 1965
Third Printing August, 1966

DEDICATION

To Gloria, Erica, Sophie and Louis—who all helped.

Library of Congress Catalog Card Number: 65-28427

Copyright © 1965 by Sylvan Fox
Afterword Copyright © 1966 by Sylvan Fox

No portion of this book may be reproduced in any form
without written permission from the Publisher, except
by a magazine or newspaper reviewer, who may quote
brief passages as part of his printed review.

AWARD BOOKS are published by
Universal Publishing and Distributing Corporation
800 Second Avenue, New York, New York 10017

Manufactured in the United States of America

TABLE OF CONTENTS

INTRODUCTION

For anyone who was fortunate enough to have been a worker on John F. Kennedy's New Frontier, there is a tendency to avoid recollection of his assassination. It all seems unreal, impossible to imagine, and, most of all, extremely painful. The pain centers about the abrupt interference with the flowering of the Country's youth. For John F. Kennedy was the embodiment of our younger generation—pulsating with new ideas and the courage to espouse them, but wise enough to be thorough in examination of past programs before seeking change, and tough enough to avoid self-deception. In his short term in office he had become the symbol of our nation's strength, hope and future. We were sure we could attain the goals he set and we hoped we could be as tireless and energetic as he was.

Nevertheless, the time has come for a dispassionate examination of the murder in Dallas. Our nation has survived the horror and the numbness has worn off. We should be prepared to exercise our critical faculties. There ought not to be any fear of stepping on toes or damaging the image of governmental agencies. You might ask, why bother? Hasn't the Warren Commission done its job? The Warren Commission has compiled a massive report, but after reading Sylvan Fox's work, I am left with many doubts about the report. How many of us could read the 26 volumes of evidence and be in a position to evaluate them? How much confidence can we have, when a thorough investigator like Mr. Fox is able to name witnesses with relevant information who were not called by the Commission?

Sylvan Fox has avoided the sensational approach, but his hard-nosed quest for information, for answers, is obviously in the highest tradition of journalism. This is not surprising in a Pulitzer-prize-winner. What is surprising and more important to me is the fact that his approach, the breadth and depth of his inquiries, are of the quality that characterizes the best and most difficult criminal investigations—those that delve into the complex relationship between racketeers and public officials.

His work has changed my mind about comfortably accepting the Warren Commission's findings.

His work will overcome your reluctance to re-examine the circumstances surrounding the assassination. It will destroy your complacency about the single-handed mentally unbalanced killer theory. It will revive your interest in the unbelievable story of Ruby's killing of Oswald in the midst of the Dallas police force. It will raise suspicions about Oswald's alleged killing of a Dallas policeman. Most of all, it raises questions that deserve to be answered concerning the possibility that a conspiracy existed to destroy President Kennedy.

This book is a challenge to our officialdom. I am sure that even before you reach the last page, you will join with Mr. Fox in seeking answers from our government. If you prefer to believe that you have been given the final answers about the assassination, don't read this book. Otherwise, you are in for an unsettling experience—and a stimulating one.

EDWYN SILBERLING
HUNTINGTON, LONG ISLAND

Foreword

At the moment that a bullet pierced the skull of John F. Kennedy in Dallas, I was sitting alone in a less than elegant restaurant called Nick's near the New York World-Telegram having lunch. The man who was then city editor of the paper had taken the day off, and I was filling in for him. The flow of news that morning had not been heavy, and I had managed to slip out for a bite to eat.

As I sipped some tea, the phone in a booth at the front of the restaurant rang. Someone answered it, leaned out of the booth and shouted: "Is there a guy named Fox from the World-Telegram here?"

I rose and walked to the phone booth, figuring that some minor crisis had developed on the city desk. Such phone calls are not uncommon on newspapers.

The call came from a girl city desk clerk, and I can remember clearly the strange urgency in her voice as she pronounced my name.

"Yes," I said with a touch of annoyance at having been called from my lunch.

"Kennedy's been shot."

"My God," I said with even greater annoyance. "Is this your idea of some kind of joke?"

"No, I mean it," she answered, sounding as though she had just run several blocks. "Kennedy's been shot."

That second time, I realized she was serious.

"Okay," I said, "I'll be right back."

I started to walk the three blocks to the paper in a kind of daze. I remember that my pace was slow at first, but accelerated as I went, and I was trotting by the time I reached the entrance to the World-Telegram building.

The atmosphere in the city room was weird. People were clustered in small knots talking quietly and looking grim.

After checking with the paper's editor, Richard D. Peters, and with its managing editor, Herb Kamm, I plunged into the job, with the other members of the staff, covering one of the most momentous and tragic events in American history. The World-Telegram produced a paper that day that remains a source of pride to all of us.

Once the job of reporting the awful events of that day and of the succeeding few days had been completed, attention focused on the commission established by President Johnson to investigate the whole shocking situation. There was a multitude of questions that had not been answered about the assassination of President Kennedy and the murder of Lee Harvey Oswald. Everyone hoped the Warren Commission would supply those answers.

Sadly, the commission did not. A host of questions remained unanswered even after the Warren Commission presented its ponderous findings.

The book that follows is not an attempt to answer all these questions. Such an attempt at this stage of history would be presumptuous.

It is, rather, an attempt to restate the questions, to point up the inconsistencies that might have remained unnoticed in earlier answers, and to take steps in the direction of the truth.

While writing this book, I was continually asked: "Who really killed Kennedy? Was Oswald really alone in this thing?" The Warren Commission Report had not given the world a convincing answer.

Thus the necessity for this book, which is based on a critical examination of the commission's findings. It was a frightening task—studying the voluminous material gathered by the commission—but an important one which I hope many others will undertake. If this book casts some rays of light in their path, my first objective will have been attained.

Chapter One

The Questions Must Be Asked

November 22, 1963, dawned gray and sullen in Dallas. There were forebodings of rain, and leaders of the factionalized Democratic party in Texas were concerned lest the weather reduce the size of the crowds that would greet President John F. Kennedy later in the day. But the sun broke through in mid-morning, and by the time the President's plane, Air Force One, had touched down at Love Field, the skies were bright and full of promise.

At the airport, a Presidential motorcade of some 21 cars and buses surrounded by a cadre of a dozen police motorcycles formed quickly for the triumphal trip into the city.

Six persons sat in the Presidential car: Secret Service agent William R. Greer was behind the wheel. At his right sat Roy H. Kellerman, a tall, graying veteran of the Secret Service who was in charge of the detail guarding the President that day. John B. Connally, the Governor of Texas, occupied a jump seat behind Kellerman. Connally's wife sat in another jump seat at her husband's left. Mrs. Jacqueline Kennedy was seated directly behind Mrs. Connally, and the President sat at his wife's right.

The route of the procession had been selected days in advance by White House aides, civic leaders, police officials and the Secret Service.

From the airport, it would take the President through

a Dallas suburb, then down into the heart of the city along busy Main Street. When the column reached Houston Street, it would make a right turn, proceed along Houston for a short distance, then make a left turn into Elm Street to mount the Stemmons Freeway for the ride to the Trade Mart, a huge convention hall where President Kennedy was to deliver a luncheon speech. The two turns, which would play such a significant role in the events that followed, were necessary to reach the Freeway, approachable along normal traffic patterns only from Elm Street.

The first forty minutes of the trip were uneventful. The motorcade made two brief stops—one so the President could sign some autographs, and a second to let him chat with a nun in the crowd. The procession was running slightly behind schedule, as most motorcades do.

As the caravan made the first of the two turns and moved slowly along crowded Houston Street, Mrs. Connally looked over her shoulder at the smiling President.

"Mr. President," she said, "you can't say Dallas doesn't love you."

President Kennedy's smile broadened in acknowledgment of the remark.

Moments after the President's car had made the second turn into Elm Street, a shot pierced the curtain of cheers engulfing the young chief. Many in the crowd turned toward a railroad overpass that lay directly ahead of the motorcade, and some began running toward it.

They were stopped by the sound of more shots. This time the firing seemed to come from behind and above the motorcade, and the attention of the terrified crowd focused on a seven-story red brick building that stands on the corner of Elm and Houston Streets.

Witnesses saw the President clutch his throat and stiffen a bit after the first shot. When the rapid series of shots—Secret Service agent Kellerman later described it as "a flurry"—had ended, the witnesses saw Kennedy topple to his left, into his wife's lap, mortally wounded.

After the first shot, Kellerman heard Mr. Kennedy

say: "My God, I am hit." Kellerman turned to see the President with both hands raised to his throat.

Mrs. Kennedy also heard the first shot. When she looked over at her husband, she noticed that his face bore a quizzical expression. Her reaction barely had time to register before she heard another shot and saw President Kennedy's skull shatter.

"Oh, my God, they have shot my husband, I have his brains in my hand," she cried, cradling the dying President in her arms. "I love you, Jack."

Governor Connally too heard the first rifle crack. "Oh no, no, no," he moaned as he realized what was happening. Then he himself was hit. "My God," he said, crumpling in his wife's arms, "they are going to kill us all."

In the front seat of the car, Kellerman responded swiftly to the tragedy unfolding behind him. "Let's get out of here," he shouted to the driver. "We are hit."

After snapping out these instructions, Kellerman got on the intercom. "We are hit," he radioed to the motorcade's lead car. "Get us to the hospital immediately."

A radio call was relayed from the lead car, notifying Parkland Hospital that the President had been shot and was being brought there. At the same time, two significant radio calls were made from the lead car.

J. E. Decker, the Dallas County sheriff, ordered his men to the railroad yards near the triple underpass that lay directly ahead of the motorcade. Jesse Curry, the Dallas police chief, instructed every available policeman in the area to surround the Texas School Book Depository, that red brick building at Elm and Houston Streets.

As the motorcade, which had slowed to about 11 miles an hour to make the turn into Elm Street, gained speed, Mrs. Kennedy played out one of the weirdest episodes in the entire drama. As if in a trance, and without evident purpose, she rose from her seat at her husband's side, climbed to the trunk of the big Lincoln, and began crawling on hands and knees across the trunk toward the back of the car. Had she fallen from the trunk as the car picked up speed, she almost certainly would have been killed.

But before this could happen, fortunately, a Secret Service man who had been riding in the followup car behind the President's, leaped to the rear of the Lincoln, intercepted Mrs. Kennedy and helped her back into her seat.

Responding to Kellerman's orders, the motorcade raced at speeds up to 80 miles an hour to Parkland Hospital, four miles away. The doctors there were ready for their distinguished patients.

President Kennedy was wheeled into an operating room where a team of medical specialists examined him. A faint heartbeat was still detectable and there was some spasmodic breathing, but no pulse. The doctors noticed two wounds—one in the front of Mr. Kennedy's neck at about the point of the knot of his tie; another, much larger, on the head.

A cursory examination of the President's back was made, and when no evidence of any serious wound was found there, the doctors assumed the throat and head wounds were the extent of the President's injury. To help Mr. Kennedy breathe, the doctors enlarged the tiny puncture in his throat and thrust a tracheotomy tube into it. But there was little that could be done about the head injury, which had blown away a large portion of the right side of Mr. Kennedy's skull and left masses of brain tissue extruding. Obviously, nothing the doctors could do would save President Kennedy's life.

At approximately 1 P.M., less than 30 minutes after President Kennedy had arrived at the hospital, Dr. William Kemp Clark, Parkland's chief neurologist, pronounced the President dead.

In another emergency room nearby, Governor Connally was treated for his wounds. Connally had been struck in the back by a bullet that cut through his chest, shattering a rib and collapsing a lung, came out the front, went through his right wrist, breaking a bone there, and lodged in his left thigh. His wounds were grave but not fatal. The Governor would recover.

Fifteen miles from the assassination scene, in suburban Irving, Lee Harvey Oswald had awakened early that morning and had left the home of Mrs. Ruth Paine, a Quaker woman who had befriended the Oswalds, before either Mrs. Paine or Oswald's Russian-born wife, Marina, had gotten up.

Oswald lived in a room in the Oak Cliff section of Dallas and normally spent only weekends at Mrs. Paine's house, where Marina and their baby daughter had been staying for two months.

But on Thursday, November 21, Oswald told Wesley Frazier, a fellow worker at the Texas School Book Depository and a neighbor of Mrs. Paine, that he was going out to Irving that night to pick up some curtain rods for his room.

As he had many times before, Frazier drove Oswald to Irving Thursday night after work, then drove him back to the book depository Friday morning. Oswald had a long brown bag with him when he got into Frazier's car that morning, and when Frazier asked him what was in it, Oswald replied: "Curtain rods."

Frazier parked the car in a company lot two blocks from the book depository and Oswald got out first, taking his package from the back seat of the car and starting across some railroad tracks toward the squat structure where they worked. Oswald usually walked along with Frazier from the parking lot, but that day he went ahead alone and was about 50 feet in front of Frazier when he entered the building.

Less than five hours later, the world heard the first stunning news of President Kennedy's assassination. As the word flashed in every newsroom and on every radio and television set in virtually every country on earth, a frantic search was already in progress for the President's assassin or assassins.

A motorcycle policeman, Marrion L. Baker, heard shots coming from the Texas School Book Depository and saw some pigeons that were perched there scatter. He rushed to the building entrance with gun drawn. There he met Roy Truly, the superintendent of the depository, who had been standing outside watching the motorcade. Together they ran up one flight of stairs to the second floor.

When he reached the landing, Baker saw a slightly built young man walking toward the far end of a lunchroom located in that part of the building. It was Lee Harvey Oswald.

"Come here," Baker shouted at the man.

As Oswald walked toward Baker, Roy Truly, who had fallen a little behind the policeman in their dash into the building, arrived on the scene. "Do you know this man, does he work here?" Baker asked Truly. "Yes," Truly replied.

Baker said later that Oswald "never did say a word or nothing," seemed calm and was not out of breath, and Truly added that Oswald "didn't seem to be excited or overly afraid or anything," beyond showing a normal concern for having Baker's revolver thrust against his abdomen.

Accepting Truly's assurances as evidence of Oswald's innocence, Baker continued up the stairs, leaving Oswald unguarded in the middle of the lunchroom. A minute later, Oswald was seen walking through some offices on the second floor. He was carrying a bottle of Coca-Cola that he apparently had bought from a vending machine in the lunchroom after his confrontation with the policeman.

Oswald left the building unmolested a few minutes later, although by this time police were swarming around and inside it.

While Oswald headed by bus, cab and on foot toward his room in the Oak Cliff section of the city, police broadcast a description of the suspected killer of the President. The description was presumably based on information supplied by an eyewitness, Howard Leslie Brennan, a 45-year-old steamfitter who had been sitting on a concrete wall directly across the street from the book depository and had reported seeing a man in the sixth-floor window fire a rifle at the President's car.

Brennan described the suspected assassin as about 30 years old, 5-foot 10-inches tall, weighing about 170 pounds.

Oswald, meanwhile, had reached his room, donned a light-colored jacket, picked up a revolver he is believed to have kept there, and left.

As he walked along the street not far from his home, a police car cruising the area pulled up near him. Oswald stopped, went over to the car and leaned inside the window on the passenger side. For a moment or so, Oswald, who had allegedly killed the President of the United States only 45 minutes earlier, seemed to talk calmly. Then Oswald drew his head out of the window and started to back away slowly.

The policeman, J. D. Tippit, opened the door on the driver's side, got out and walked toward the front of the car. As he reached the front left wheel, Oswald drew a revolver and fired four bullets into Tippit, killing him on the spot.

Oswald then headed down the street in the direction from which he had come. As he went, he was heard to mutter, "poor dumb cop," or "poor damn cop."

After stopping in doorways once or twice, apparently to avoid being seen by cruising police, Oswald ducked into a movie theater where he was arrested by policemen who had traced him there through information provided by witnesses to the Tippit shooting and Oswald's flight.

For the second time in barely an hour, Oswald was approached by a policeman with gun drawn. It had happened just moments after the assassination when Patrolman Marrion Baker had rushed up to Oswald in the book depository. Oswald had remained calm and relaxed then. This time it was different.

"Well, it is all over now," Oswald said. And, according to the police involved, Oswald drew his gun, tried unsuccessfully to fire it, then lashed out with his fists and had to be forcibly subdued.

During the ensuing police interrogations, Oswald steadfastly and repeatedly denied he had shot either the President or Tippit. At first, he was charged only with the murder of the policeman. Hours later, however, he was booked for the slaying of Kennedy as well.

On Sunday, November 24, the violence that had gripped Dallas and the nation for two days spilled over in one final eruption before the eyes of millions of horrified television viewers.

As Oswald was being led to a car in the basement of the Dallas police headquarters, preparatory to being moved to more permanent accommodations in the county jail, a stocky man well known to many Dallas policemen darted from the crowd of newsmen and police that had gathered there and fired a single shot into Oswald's abdomen. Oswald slipped to the floor with a groan, lost consciousness, and was pronounced dead at Parkland Hospital a short time later.

Oswald's killer, a Dallas nightclub owner named Jack Ruby, was seized immediately. His only explanation for the shooting was that he wanted to spare Mrs. Kennedy the ordeal of testifying at Oswald's trial.

Except for Ruby's trial, which shed little new light on the events in Dallas, the drama had ended. The American people had witnessed an orgy of violence and a breakdown of law and order unparalleled in their history.

There remained, however, the task of organizing these events into an official record, for Jack Ruby, and the negligence of the Dallas police, had closed the door forever on the normal process of justice which might have provided such a record of the full story of the assassination.

As one of his first official acts, Lyndon B. Johnson, the new President, ordered the creation of a Presidential Commission to investigate the assassination of President Kennedy and the subsequent murder of Lee Harvey

Oswald, and to issue a full report of its findings. Johnson designated Chief Justice Earl Warren to head the Commission. The other members were Senators Richard B. Russell and John Sherman Cooper; Representatives Hale Boggs and Gerald Ford; Allen W. Dulles and John J. McCloy.

Russell is a Democrat from Georgia and a staunch spokesman for the Southern wing of his party. Cooper, a former ambassador to India, is a liberal Republican from Kentucky. Boggs is a conservative Southern Democrat from Louisiana, and Ford is also a conservative Republican from Michigan. Dulles gained fame as the head of the super-secret Central Intelligence Agency during the Eisenhower administration, and McCloy is a banker who had served as an adviser to President Kennedy.

The composition of the Commission caused debate. Many felt it was too heavily weighted with right-wing and Southern sentiment. Its completely political nature was highly criticized. Why, some observers asked, were all the members of the Commission drawn from the ranks of those intimately involved in the affairs of the United States government? Why were there no disinterested members—a distinguished lawyer, for example, or one of the nation's leading historians, or a prominent psychiatrist?

The Commission's actions, even before it issued its Report also came under severe fire, especially because stories about its work and its ultimate findings "leaked" to favored newspapers despite the statements of some Commission members that nothing would be revealed until the Report was released.

Relying almost entirely in its investigation on the Federal Bureau of Investigation and the Secret Service, the Commission conducted closed hearings—in all but one case—and took testimony or depositions from 552 witnesses, ranging from President Johnson to the house-keeper in Lee Oswald's rooming house. On Sept. 24, 1964, the Commission issued its report.

The Commission's findings contained no surprises; Lee Harvey Oswald killed President Kennedy and was in turn killed by Jack Ruby, the Commission said, and each acted alone, without the aid or support of co-conspirators or accomplices, so far as the Commission was able to determine.

The Report was greeted in the United States with what amounted to a national sigh of relief. Americans, grown tense and edgy with the suspicion that the assassination was merely the top of an iceberg that plunged far below the surface, breathed easier again. Illustrative of this attitude are the comments of Louis Nizer, the estimable New York lawyer who has gained fame and fortune acting as counsel to a host of Hollywood and Broadway personalities.

In the preface to one edition of the Report, Nizer in effect expresses the view that the Warren Commission's findings are tantamount to Gospel and that reasonable men henceforth will accept them on faith. This seems surprising from a lawyer of Nizer's repute.

Some American commentators and many distinguished European historians and journalists approached the Report more critically. They challenged some of the Commission's findings, expressed doubt about others, questioned some of the Commission's method's of seeking the truth. A "Who Killed Kennedy?" committee was organized in Britain. Headed by such notable figures as Bertrand Russell, Hugh Trevor-Roper, the Oxford professor of modern history, Tony Richardson, the movie producer, and Kenneth Tynan, the writer and critic, the committee launched its own investigation of the Dallas affair, expressing the view that the Warren Commission's findings were not adequately substantiated.

Like the leaders of the "Who Killed Kennedy?" committee, many in this country and abroad called the summation deduced by the Commission a little too pat to be entirely acceptable. They were bothered by the number of unanswered questions that cropped up insistently during examination of the Report.

It is reasonable to assume that the Commission provided the American people with all the information it was able to provide about the assassination—or at least with all the information it believed itself able to provide. The American people, and the people of the world, however, are clearly entitled to ask questions and to attempt to obtain answers where possible. It is their right and their responsibility to scrutinize, to criticize, and to challenge any government document of this kind.

Historians will ask and re-ask pertinent questions about John F. Kennedy's death for years to come. They will criticize the Commission for its shortcomings and failings. They will doubt and they will seek to resolve their doubts. This is the way an event of the magnitude of President Kennedy's assassination is understood, and to insist, as some do, that no questions be asked is to slam the door on critical thought about one of the most momentous and appalling tragedies in the nation's history.

The questions are there—and in the succeeding chapters of this book, they will be asked.

Chapter Two

The Question of Motive

Motive is an essential element of virtually every crime. With rare exceptions, crimes are committed for a reason. Some are committed for financial gain, some for revenge, some with a political objective in mind. To understand a crime, whether it is the assassination of a President or the theft of a car, one must understand the motive that impelled that crime. To exclude this element is to fail to tell the full story, to fail to answer the crucial question: Why?

Only occasionally is a crime committed senselessly and without purpose. The perpetrator in such a case is deranged and his motivation in committing the crime lies deep within his distorted mind, usually beyond the reach of rational people. This is rare, however.

More frequently, the man who commits a seemingly senseless or incomprehensible crime is adjudged deranged after he has performed the criminal act. Up to the time of the crime, he was considered rational and sane; only the crime itself establishes him as irrational and demented. Something suddenly snaps, the advocates of this approach to criminal psychology would have us believe.

Too often, this last category has become a catch-all. When an inadequate investigation fails to turn up a reasonable explanation for a crime, when investigators are unable to establish a clear motive, the criminal is tossed into that classification of suddenly deranged persons who commit inexplicable crimes after living exemplary, or at least normal, lives. Such crimes do occur, of course, but far less frequently than many official records would suggest. More often, the suddenly deranged person either has, it later turns out, a history of mental illness that has been held under control, or he has a comprehensible motive for his act.

Psychiatrists are understandably wary of this "sudden snap" theory. They know that the processes of mental breakdown are relatively slow in most cases and that derangement so extreme as to express itself in murder rarely occurs overnight. As in most diseases, the symptoms of psychosis can be detected and its course can often be predicted. Remarkably few insane or purposeless murders are committed by persons who were previously unknown to the police or to a psychiatrist. Almost invariably, the murderer has a record of developing derangement and the outburst of violence that culminates in murder can then be seen as a logical step in the course of the killer's illness.

Implicit in the Warren Commission's conclusions is the thesis that Lee Harvey Oswald killed the President for obscure reasons stemming from some extreme derangement, and that Jack Ruby killed Oswald out of a similar irrational motivation. Thus, the Commission suggests, two of the principal players in one of history's greatest tragedies were men who simply went berserk.

"To determine the motives for the assassination of President Kennedy," the Report states, "one must look to the assassin himself. Clues to Oswald's motives can be found in his family history, his education or lack of it, his acts, his writings, and the recollection of those who had close contacts with him throughout his life ... The Commission could not make any definitive determination of Oswald's motives."

In other words, on the vital question of motive, the Commission is frankly inconclusive and suggests that "others may study Lee Oswald's life and arrive at their own conclusions as to his possible motives."

Such a statement leaves a large and haunting question: Accepting entirely for the moment the conclusion that Oswald killed President Kennedy and did it alone, why did he do it? Did his purported derangement somehow focus on Kennedy? There is no evidence to support an affirmative reply. Did he see Mr. Kennedy as somehow causing his personal difficulties? There is nothing to support such a theory either. Did he conceive of Mr. Kennedy, in some paranoiac nightmare, as his persecutor? Nothing suggests that this is likely.

In fact, the whole system that assumes that the assassination grew out of some form of derangement is difficult indeed to substantiate. It is just as reasonable to assume from the available evidence that Oswald had some undiscerned but completely comprehensible reason for killing President Kennedy as it is to decide, on the basis of psychological study of Oswald after his death, that he acted irrationally.

The Commission's attempt to interpret clues to Oswald's motives relies upon a method that might be called psychoanalysis *a posteriori*. It is a technique by which almost anything can be proved about almost anyone, depending upon the selection of psychological data.

In its effort to determine Oswald's motives, the Commission, which had a staff that included neither a psychiatrist nor a psychologist, presents a detailed biographical study of Oswald constructed in psychiatric terms, a psychological post-mortem which pieces together bits of information supplied by acquaintances, relatives, investigators and co-workers, all of whom knew that Oswald was alleged to have killed the President when they testified about his past behavior.

Based on this information, the Commission drew up a list of "factors" which "might have influenced" Oswald's decision to assassinate the President. Here is that list:

"(a) His deep-rooted resentment of all authority

which was expressed in a hostility toward every society in which he lived;

"(b) His inability to enter into meaningful relationships with people, and a continuous pattern of rejecting his environment in favor of new surroundings;

"(c) His urge to try to find a place in history and despair at times over his failures in his various undertakings;

"(d) His capacity for violence as evidenced by his attempts to kill General Walker;

"(e) His avowed commitment to Marxism and communism, as he understood the terms and developed his own interpretation of them; this was expressed by his antagonism toward the United States, by his defection to the Soviet Union, by his failure to be reconciled with life in the United States even after his disenchantment with the Soviet Union, and by his efforts, though frustrated, to go to Cuba."

"Each of these," the Commission adds, "contributed to his capacity to risk all in cruel and irresponsible action."

These are interesting hypothetical ingredients at best. Not one of them is a substantive motive—nor really even suggests a substantive motive—for the crime. They still leave unanswered the question of *why* Oswald killed Kennedy.

There are doubtless hundreds, perhaps even thousands, of men living in the United States today who have a deep-rooted resentment of authority, an inability to enter into meaningful relationships, an urge to find a place in history, a capacity for violence, and even an avowed commitment to Marxism and communism as they understand the terms.

Yet they did not assassinate the President, nor are they likely to do so. Some will live unhappy lives, work at drab jobs, marry, have children, leave their wives—just as Oswald did all these things. But the chances are slim that they will kill.

Oswald was somehow different. Either he fit all of these descriptions and was psychotic as well, or he had a reason to kill Kennedy. The factors provided by the Commission, by themselves, simply cannot be said to add up to the picture of a Presidential assassin.

All the evidence presented by the Commission and available from any other sources suggests that Oswald was sane, in both the legal and the medical sense, at the time of the assassination. The Commission's awareness of this fact poses a serious problem for, in its Report, the Commission never says Oswald was insane, yet it speculates about his motives in the terminology of psychiatry.

The earliest testimony to Oswald's mental condition was given by Dr. Renatus Hartogs, the chief psychiatrist at Youth House in New York, a detention center for wayward youngsters, where Oswald, as a truant, was examined by Hartogs.

"I found him to be a medium-sized, slender, curly-haired youngster, pale-faced, who was not very talkative. ...not very responsive. He had to be prompted," Hartogs told the Warren Commission. "He was polite. He answered in a somewhat monotonous fashion. His sentences were well-structured. He was in full contact with reality."

This last comment surprised Wesley J. Liebler, an assistant counsel to the Commission, who apparently had been expecting Hartogs to describe the young Oswald as an incipient psychotic.

"He was?" Liebler asked.

"He was in full contact with reality," Hartogs repeated firmly.

Later in his testimony, Hartogs entered into the record the written report on Oswald prepared at Youth House. It describes a clearly troubled boy, the product of a broken home, with a mother handicapped in rearing her child. But it concluded unequivocally that "psychotic mental content was denied and no indication of psychotic mental changes were arrived at." In the judgment of competent and qualified psychiatrists who examined Oswald when he was 13 years of age, he was not psychotic.

The Commission goes even further in evidence that at this point in his life, Oswald showed no signs of becoming a deranged assassin. Referring to Hartogs' testimony, the Commission declared:

"Contrary to reports that appeared after the assassination, the psychiatric examination did not indicate that Lee Oswald was a potential assassin, potentially dangerous, that 'his outlook on life had strongly paranoid overtones,' or that he should be institutionalized."

Perhaps then Oswald became deranged some time during the next 10 or 11 years, if the Commission's suppositions to his reasons for killing the President are correct. The evidence seems to suggest otherwise.

There is little doubt that Oswald was a disturbed youngster. His life during the 11 years that remained of it never contradicts that premise. But there are important differences between unstable, neurotic people and psychotics. A psychotic—a person out of touch with reality—might kill without purpose or reason. "God told me to do it," he might say afterward, or "now the world will be safe." A disturbed neurotic probably would need a good reason to kill; having been provided with such a reason, he might be capable of killing. Such a man probably would have a clear idea of the reason behind his action.

Although psychotic symptoms are absent in Oswald, there is a wealth of evidence showing him to be a strange, unstable, paradoxical young man.

After his release from Youth House, his mother took him back to New Orleans, the city of his birth. He returned to school for a while, and when he was about 15 became interested in Marxism. Upon completing the ninth grade, Oswald quit school and got a job. He praised Khrushchev to a fellow employee, suggested they join the Communist Party—something Oswald never did, by the way—and once told him he would like to kill President Eisenhower because he was exploiting the working class.

Despite this interest in communism and Marxism, Oswald tried to join the Marines when he was 16 years old. He was rejected because of his age. But a year later, when he was 17, Oswald tried again. This time he was accepted.

The Report passes over this event with little significant comment. But it is worth noting that applicants for enlistment in any branch of the armed forces are tested and examined to determine whether they are fit to withstand the rigors of military life and to accept the discipline it requires. In addition, the Marine Corps has always prided itself on being by far the most selective of the services. Assuming Oswald was subjected to the usual enlistment testing, and there is no reason to suspect that he was not, it seems obvious that at the time he was 17 he certainly was not manifestly psychotic nor even in a highly disturbed neurotic state. Else he would have been rejected by the Marine Corps, as thousands who never become presidential assassins are each year.

The Report confirms this: ". . . . There is nothing in Oswald's military records to indicate that he was mentally unstable or otherwise psychologically unfit for duty in the Marine Corps . . ."

After serving in the Marine Corps for almost three years, Oswald requested a transfer from active duty to reserve status. He said he wanted to leave the Corps three months before his enlistment expired to care for his mother, who had been injured in an accident. He was granted an honorable discharge. (This was later changed to an undesirable discharge, but only because Oswald had defected to the Soviet Union, not for any failure to function as a Marine.)

Thus, at the age of 20, Oswald left the Marine Corps certifiably sane and without any overt or even suspected psychotic tendencies. Nor does subsequent information suggest that Oswald is a man undergoing psychotic changes of personality.

After returning to civilian life, Oswald defected to Russia and lived there for a few months short of three years. While there, he reportedly attempted suicide when the Russian authorities at first refused to permit him to remain in the country. This could be an alarming symptom of possible mental breakdown. But Soviet psychiatrists who examined him at the time found him sane; and upon his return to the United States, he was kept under close scrutiny by the FBI, and its records show nothing to suggest any further hint of psychosis.

James P. Hosty Jr., the FBI agent assigned to Oswald's case at the time of the assassination, told the Warren Commission he was astonished to learn that Oswald was being held for the murder of the President.

"What was your reaction?" Hosty was asked during his appearance before the Commission.

"Shock, complete surprise," he said. "I had no reason prior to this time to believe that he was capable or potentially an assassin of the President of the United States. ... Prior to the assassination of the President of the United States, I had no information indicating violence on the part of Lee Harvey Oswald."

The final clue to Oswald's mental condition must be sought in his behavior after his arrest. Was he irrational then, or out of touch with reality? Had something snapped during the 24 or 48 hours immediately preceding the assassination?

There is nothing to indicate that his behavior had changed in any significant way. Accounts of his interrogation do not suggest that he was incoherent or unaware of what was happening to him. He denied any role in the assassination of Kennedy or the shooting of Officer Tippit, and he requested legal counsel—both the acts of a reasonably rational man who realizes the nature of his plight.

"I think," said Capt. J. W. Fritz, the head of the Dallas Police Department's homicide bureau and the man who conducted Oswald's interrogation after the assassination, "he was a person who had his mind made up what he was going to do and I think he was like a person just dedicated to a cause.

"I know a lot of people call him a nut all the time," Fritz added, "but he didn't talk like a nut."

The inevitable conclusion then is that Oswald was sane at the time of the assassination. And if he was sane, he must have had some reason—comprehensible even if unacceptable to the rest of us—for killing the President. You cannot have both sides of it.

Either the assassin was insane, went completely berserk and killed for some incomprehensible reason, or he was sane—however unstable and disturbed—and he killed for a cogent reason the Warren Commission failed to ascertain.

If Oswald was indeed sane, what possible reasons could have impelled him to assassinate President Kennedy?

Obviously, any attempts to answer this question would be conjectural, since the question never can be answered with certainty on the basis of the information the Commission has obtained. Nevertheless, such conjecture could conceivably be as valid as the Commission's speculative list of contributory "factors," so let us, at the Commission's invitation, play the game.

What emerges from a study of Oswald's life is the strong impression of a young man searching for a political cause. Coupled with this is the inescapably contradictory character of much of his life.

First he became interested in Marxism. A short time later, he joined the Marine Corps, an institution highly antagonistic to Marxist thought. He defected to the Soviet Union, but soon grew to despise life there and returned to the United States. Later, he became interested in the Castro revolution in Cuba. And there is even some evidence to suggest that he also became interested in the anti-Castro underground in New Orleans. His first overt act of violence was aimed at Gen. Edwin A. Walker. His second was aimed at President Kennedy.

As one of its "factors," the Commission cites Oswald's attempts on the life of General Walker. It cites this as significant not of Oswald's political preoccupation, but of his capacity for violence.

General Walker is a political right-winger who was ordered home from a command post in Germany by President Kennedy in 1962 because of the charge that the General was indoctrinating his troops with John Birch

Society material. Since taking up residence in Dallas, Walker has become identified with right-wing causes. During attempts to register a Negro student at the University of Mississippi, Walker was accused of leading a riotous band of protesters and was arrested for inciting to insurrection, a charge that was later dropped.

Walker is surrounded by a group of fervent young supporters who served with him in Germany. One of Walker's adherents is Bernard Weissman, who was in Dallas on the day of Kennedy's assassination and who placed the advertisement attacking Kennedy in the Dallas Morning News the day the President was killed.

Because Walker has become a symbol of ultra-rightist thinking in this country, an attempt on his life by a total stranger would almost inevitably be politically inspired.

Oswald's attempt to assassinate Walker was planned, according to information provided by Oswald's wife, Marina. He took photographs of Walker's house and the surrounding neighborhood. He postponed the day of the attempt when he learned that a crowd would be attending a meeting at a nearby church a few days later, making it easier for him to slip in and out of the neighborhood undetected. He planned his escape.

If Marina Oswald is correct, this was a carefully worked out assassination plot with a clear political motivation.

But if Walker was politically obnoxious to Oswald, how could John F. Kennedy, a liberal Democrat, also be Oswald's political enemy?

To an American, whose political orientation lies within a fairly narrow spectrum, *this seems to be an impossible contradiction.* But the world of November, 1963, was a complex one. Left-wing and Communist parties had been torn apart by a massive internal dispute between Moscow and Peking. The result was a splintering of left-wing groups and the emergence of new extremist elements.

From the low ebb of the Cuban missile crisis in October, 1961, relations between the United States and the Soviet Union had steadily improved. But while Washington and Moscow were seeking further rapproachments, these left-wing extremist groups were attempting to undermine the new spirit of co-existence that prevailed.

In their view, Khrushchev and Kennedy, each in his own way and for his own reasons, were together thwarting the forces of revolution and communism. These extremists turned for their guidance to Peking—and to that shining beacon of communist revolution in the Western Hemisphere, Havana.

The Progressive Labor Movement is a typical product of this bitter splintering process on the left. Its leaders were members of the American Communist Party until the struggle between Moscow and Peking began. Expelled from the party for siding with Mao, they formed a new organization more radical and more willing to resort to violence than the Communist Party ever was.

From its creation, the PLM proclaimed itself the champion of Castro and the Cuban revolution. It organized trips to Cuba in defiance of the State Department's travel bans, and it infiltrated the Fair Play For Cuba Committee.

Oswald too was disillusioned with the Soviet Union. And Oswald too adopted the Cuban revolution as his new cause.

To the PLM, and to Oswald, there was little difference between a rightist like General Walker and a liberal Democrat like President Kennedy. Both were enemies of revolutionary socialist progress. Both were enemies of Castro.

There is no evidence to suggest that Oswald actually was a member of the PLM or even knew of its existence, although there is no evidence either to suggest that any investigation along these lines was ever undertaken by the Warren Commission. But there is an abundance of evidence to suggest that the same ideological forces that created the PLM and other groups like it around the world at this time also created the motivation that led

Oswald to try to kill Walker and to succeed in killing Mr. Kennedy.

Nowhere does the Commission explain why it so thoroughly ignores the important political aspects of Oswald's life and personality, choosing instead to focus on his upbringing and his inability to form meaningful relationships. The political significance of Mr. Kennedy's assassination would appear to have been a far more fruitful area of speculation for the Commission than the complex, undecipherable psychological convolutions of a dead assassin. Rather than hypothesizing on Oswald's capacity for violence, the Commission might well have considered the possibility, even the probability, that Oswald killed Mr. Kennedy out of some belief that he was accomplishing an important political mission.

There is another conjectural explanation for Oswald's motive which hinges on the possibility—suggested by a great deal of interesting evidence and testimony—that Oswald was during the last few years of his life an informer or agent of the CIA, the FBI or both.

It should be stated at the outset that the Warren Commission vigorously denies that Oswald was in the employ of any agency of the United States government, or any other government for that matter.

Despite these disclaimers, the record discloses a number of curious items.

First there are the circumstances surrounding Oswald's defection to Russia and his subsequent return. Although Oswald went to the Soviet Union and there tried to renounce his American citizenship, and although he may well have supplied the Russians with valuable electronic and radar information he picked up while a Marine, the United States government acted singularly unconcerned. Oswald was never arrested or prosecuted for espionage or any other crime growing out of his defection.

Some time later, while handing out pro-Castro leaflets on a New Orleans street, Oswald got into a fight with a group of anti-Castro Cubans and was arrested by the New Orleans police for disturbing the peace. After being held in jail overnight, Oswald "asked the New Orleans police to arrange for him to be interviewed by the FBI." The police agreed, called the local FBI office, and agent John L. Quigley visited Oswald at the police station.

This, to say the least, is an unusual request for a staunch pro-Castro Marxist to make. But the Warren Commission offers no explanation of why Oswald wanted to see an FBI agent at the New Orleans police station.

Still later, Oswald applied for a passport, listing his destination, among other places, as Poland and the Soviet Union. Actually, as events later revealed, he really hoped to go to Cuba.

Despite the fact that he was a known defector who had attempted to renounce his American citizenship, a man who had returned to the United States only to engage in pro-Castro activities, *Oswald was given a passport in 24 hours!*

If Oswald was in fact working for the CIA or the FBI, the entire picture we have of him as a leftist and a pro-Castroite is a fiction.

Regardless of how Oswald is seen, he is clearly a man deeply involved in political extremism.

If Oswald was a politically preoccupied man, Jack Ruby appears to be the opposite. He seems to have had no pronounced political beliefs at any time in his life.

Ruby insisted throughout his trial for Oswald's murder and during his testimony to the Warren Commission that he killed Oswald on impulse and that his sole purpose was to spare Mrs. Kennedy the ordeal of testifying at Oswald's trial. Only if we accept the idea that Ruby is insane can we accept such an explanation as the motive for the murder.

Again we are faced with the necessity of accepting madness where there is no prior evidence of it. There is nothing to indicate that Ruby was insane before he killed Oswald. In this connection, some portions of Ruby's testimony to the Warren Commission are worth looking at closely.

At one point in his testimony, Ruby insisted that

Sheriff Decker and other local lew-enforcement officials leave the hearing room. After they had left, Ruby said:

"Gentlemen, if you want to hear any further testimony, you will have to get me to Washington soon, because it has something to do with you, Chief Warren."

A moment later, Ruby added:

"I want to tell the truth, and I can't tell it here. I can't tell it here. Does that make sense to you?"

And still later:

"But this isn't the place for me to tell what I want to tell. . . . Chief Warren, your life is in danger in this city, you know that?"

Ruby went on to assert that his whole family was in danger of being killed, and when Warren pointed out that one of Ruby's sisters had written to the Commission asking that Ruby be called to testify, Ruby reminded Warren that the letter was sent two or three months earlier, and said:

"At that time, when you first got the letter and I was begging Joe Tonahill (Ruby's lawyer) and the other lawyers to know the truth about me, certain things that are happening now wouldn't be happening at this particular time."

"Yes?" Warren asked.

"Because then they would have known the truth about Jack Ruby and his emotional breakdown."

"Yes?" Warren asked again.

"Of why that Sunday morning—that thought never entered my mind prior to that Sunday morning when I took it upon myself to try to be a martyr or some screwball, you might say.

"But I felt very emotional and very carried away for Mrs. Kennedy, that with all the strife she had gone through—I had been following it pretty well—that someone owed it to our beloved President that she shouldn't be expected to come back to face trial of this heinous crime.

"And I never had the chance to tell that, to back it up, to prove it.

"Consequently, right at this moment I am being victimized as part of a plot in the world's worst tragedy and crime at this moment.... At this moment Lee Harvey Oswald isn't guilty of committing the crime of assassinating President Kennedy. Jack Ruby is."

Warren withheld comment on Ruby's suggestion that he is somehow being blamed for the assassination, and Ruby went on:

"There is an organization here, Chief Justice Warren, if it takes my life at this moment to say it, and Bill Decker said be a man and say it ..... take that for what it is worth, Chief Justice Warren.

"Unfortunately for me, for me giving the people the opportunity to get in power, because of the act I committed, has put a lot of people in jeopardy with their lives."

Ruby paused momentarily, then said:

"Don't register with you, does it?"

Are these the ravings of a madman, or some feeble effort on Ruby's part to tell the Commission more than he feels safely able to reveal?

Several aspects of this faltering testimony are interesting. First, Ruby refused to say any of these things until after the local law-enforcement officials had left the hearing room. Ruby obviously believed, rationally or not, he had some reason to fear making such statements in their presence.

Ruby then said that if the Commission had not waited several months to hear his testimony, "certain things that are happening to me now wouldn't be happening at this particular time."

What does Ruby mean by this? The Warren Commission does not ask him, nor does it pursue his next comment:

"Because then they would have known the truth about Jack Ruby and his emotional breakdown."

From an insane man, we can accept the story of a murder to spare a widow the pain of attending the trial of her husband's killer. Such a story told by a sane man can only be seen as a feeble cover for the truth. The implication of much of Ruby's testimony is that he is telling this story out of fear for the safety of his family, that revealing the truth about his murder of Oswald would bring swift retribution to everyone close to him.

"I tell you, gentlemen," he said to the Warren Commission, "my whole family is in jeopardy. . . . as to their lives."

In formulating its conclusions, the Commission constructed this logical system:

1—Oswald killed Kennedy, and Ruby killed Oswald.

2—There was no conspiracy; each acted entirely on his own.

3—Oswald had no discernible rational motive.

4—Therefore, Ruby had no rational motive.

Only if Oswald killed Kennedy for a reason could Ruby have had some rational reason for killing Oswald. What possible motive might Ruby have had?

One answer springs to mind immediately: Ruby killed Oswald to silence him and prevent him from ever appearing at a trial.

This hypothesis depends heavily on the existence of a conspiracy, and the Warren Commission rejects that premise, so automatically it rejects the possibility that Ruby acted with the purpose of preventing Oswald from revealing something about the assassination.

There is some question about whether Ruby knew Oswald, although obviously this is not a necessary condition for the existence of a conspiracy. They lived less than a mile apart, had post-office boxes only a few feet apart, yet they need not have been acquainted to be involved in a plot to kill the President. In a well-constructed plot, few of the principals would know each other, and the contacts linking the conspirators would be limited to one or two persons.

Chapter Three

Was There A Conspiracy?

Put this question to almost any casual reader of newspapers or viewer of television newscasts: Did the Warren Commission declare that there was no conspiracy involved in either the assassination of President Kennedy or the murder of Lee Oswald?

The answer almost invariably will be yes.

That answer, like many that are given about the Report by those who have received their information second-hand, is incorrect and betrays a dangerous misconception of the Commission's findings.

Precisely what did the Commission say about this question of conspiracy?

"The Commission has FOUND NO EVIDENCE that either Lee Harvey Oswald or Jack Ruby was part of any conspiracy, domestic or foreign, to assassinate President Kennedy...."

The Commission then adds this important cautionary word:

"Because of the difficulty of proving negatives to a certainty, the possibility of others being involved with either Oswald or Ruby cannot be established categorically, but if there is any such evidence, it has been beyond the reach of all the investigative agencies and resources of the United States and has not come to the attention of this Commission."

38

This paragraph is subject for closer scrutiny. The presumable intent of the sentence is: "Because of the difficulty of proving negatives to a certainty, the possibility of others being involved with either Oswald or Ruby cannot be DENIED categorically...."

As the sentence reads in the text, it suggests that the Commission was unable to establish to a certainty that others WERE involved in the assassination, implying thereby that the Commission may have believed in fact that others were involved but simply was unable to prove these suspicions. Is this an error in sentence structure— or a Freudian slip?

In any case, just as the Commission confessed to its inability to discover *why* Oswald killed Mr. Kennedy, so too does it appear to admit that it cannot declare without qualification that the assassination of Mr. Kennedy or the slaying of Oswald—or both—were not the work of conspiratorial groups.

Before looking at the substance of the evidence in the Report dealing with possible conspiracy, let us look briefly at some aspects of conspiracy in general.

By the Commission's definition, if one other person was involved with either Oswald or Ruby, a conspiracy existed. The absence of a single accomplice, before or after the fact, is the necessary condition for the absence of a conspiracy.

Obviously, a plot to assassinate the President of the United States or a plot to kill the President's assassin would be difficult indeed to trace. Conspirators do not make it easy for "investigative agencies" to locate them and link them with the plot. In addition, it can be assumed that the conspirators in a plot to assassinate the President would make themselves thoroughly familiar with the workings of all federal and local investigative agencies and would take great pains to elude or confuse them.

Their task would be facilitated by the reluctance of these agencies to make themselves look bad, and by the determination of these agencies not to undermine public confidence in them or admit their own immense failures.

Avoiding detection would be made still easier by an investigative body which hoped before it started its investigation, as did most of America's political establishment, that it would not discover any conspiracy reaching into the fabric of the nation. Such a discovery, had it been made, would have created new crises in the society possibly even greater than the crises that surrounded the death of the President.

For example, let us suppose that there were persons who believed it essential to remove President Kennedy from office and that they organized an assassination plot. The discovery of such a plot, rife with political implication, would have posed a greater threat to the nation's stability than the assassination itself. One of the major sources of pride in the United States during the bleak days that followed President Kennedy's death was the calm and efficient way in which political power was transferred without strife or upheaval.

Had the Commission discovered, to offer another example, that Oswald was the trigger man in a leftist plot, the wave of anti-Communist hysteria resulting from such a discovery would have made the McCarthy era seem tepid by comparison. And the impact of such a revelation on the nation's foreign policy might well have changed the course of history.

Similarly, if the Commission deduced that Oswald acted as the agent of ultra-rightists, the American people, normally moderate in their political tone, might well have turned violent and radical in reaction.

The Commission's assignment was to investigate the assassination and to report its findings to the American people. It could understandably have been predisposed to hope that its findings would not shake the foundations of American society and touch off new dissension and chaos.

Remember, the Commission does not say there was no

conspiracy, although it tries vigorously to appear to be saying precisely that. It says only that it could find no evidence of a conspiracy, which immediately raises the question: Did it look hard enough and go far enough?

In deciding it could find no conspiracy, the Commission appears to turn its back on a wealth of evidence suggesting that a plot—or even two separate plots—may have been operative in the deaths of John F. Kennedy and Lee Harvey Oswald. It appears to have rejected this evidence either because it was unable to corroborate it or because it was unwilling to pursue it. But in view of the vital importance involved, is this good enough reason? On close examination, much of this evidence is suggestive, and some is shocking.

Perhaps the most shocking bit of information in the entire report of the Warren Commission is the disclosure that no records exist of Oswald's interrogation by the police, the FBI and the Secret Service. Equally appalling is the Commission's apparently noncommital acceptance of the absence of such records.

Between the time Oswald was arrested shortly before 2 p.m. on November 22 and the time he was shot at 11:21 a.m. on November 24, Oswald was questioned for a total of 12 hours by Capt. J. W. Fritz, the head of the Dallas Police Department's homicide and robbery bureau.

The Warren Report concedes that there are no stenographic records of these interrogations, nor are there any tape recordings, and it declares that Fritz "kept no notes." The Report does not say Fritz "made no notes" or "took no notes," is says he "kept no notes." (The report's wording suggests that Fritz disposed of his notes.)

On checking further, we find that this appears to be what happened. Appended to the Report is a reproduction of a 13-page typewritten memorandum submitted to the Commission by Fritz. It contains considerable detail about questions Fritz asked, and answers Oswald gave. On the last page, in the last paragraph, Fritz says: "Inasmuch as this report was made from rough notes and memory, it is entirely possible that one of these questions could be in a separate interview from the one indicated in this report."

In other words, Fritz did make notes but apparently disposed of them after composing his 13-page report for the Commission.

The Warren Commission explains Fritz's actions by saying he "kept no notes." The Commission stolidly refuses to tell what really happened—that Fritz took notes and then disposed of them.

This is a truly remarkable situation. The police of a large city arrest a man suspected of having assassinated the President of the United States. They question him for a total of 12 hours. Yet not one verbatim record of that questioning survives.

In the normal course of a police interrogation, as everyone knows, the police are required to warn a suspect that anything he says may be taken down and used in evidence against him. We are assured by the Warren Commission that Oswald was given this warning soon after his arrest. How the Dallas police were planning to use what Oswald said against him if they never recorded what he said, we are not told.

How reliable is Capt. Fritz's report on Oswald's interrogation? There is at least one error, even in this carefully composed document prepared by Fritz and checked by him before its submission to the Warren Commission. On page 4 of Fritz's statement, he says:

"At 7:05 p.m. I signed a complaint before Bill Alexander of the District Attorney's office, charging Oswald with the Tippit murder. At 7:10 p.m. Tippit was arraigned before Judge Johnson."

According to this sworn statement on Oswald's interrogation prepared by the chief of the Dallas Police Department's homicide bureau, a dead policeman was arraigned before a Dallas judge that night.

Now this may be trivial and excusable in light of the pressure and excitement, but it points up the importance of keeping original documents and notes.

Oswald did not live long enough to appear in a court-room and tell his story, as he might have done if he had ever come to trial. The only record of what Oswald said about his part in the assassination would have been embodied in the verbatim transcript of his interrogation, which Oswald himself could have read, corrected and initialed. But we learn from the Warren Commission that such a transcript does not exist.

What police department in a civilized nation would be expected to operate this way? We cannot ascribe the absence of any record of the interrogation to mere care-lessness. Police may be sloppy at times in routine cases, but they are unlikely to be this careless in the immensity of a case involving the murder of a President.

The Commission takes solace from the fact that those present at the interrogations of Oswald "usually in-cluded" FBI men and Secret Service agents. In fact, only one FBI man, James Bookhout, was consistently present, and there is no indication that he attended every inter-rogation session.

Without a transcript of the questions and answers, we have no way of determining what ground was cov-ered by Captain Fritz, who by the Commission's own admission did "most of the questioning."

The Warren Report says that the police who arrested Oswald at the Texas Theater brought him to Police Headquarters at about 2 p.m. Oswald, the Report says, was taken immediately to the third-floor offices of the homicide and robbery bureau to await the arrival of Captain Fritz, who had been directing the investigation at the Texas School Book Depository.

"After about 15 or 20 minutes," the Reports says, "Os-wald was ushered into the offices of Captain Fritz for the first of several interrogation sessions. At 4:05 p.m. he was taken to the basement assembly room for his first lineup. While waiting outside the lineup room, Oswald was searched and five cartridges and other items were removed from his pockets."

Two things are interesting about this comment. First, it makes clear that Oswald and Fritz were together for about an hour before any federal agents—either FBI or Secret Service—arrived to join in the interrogation. FBI men Hosty and Bookhout reached Fritz's office, according to their statements to the Commission at 3:15 p.m. This means that during the first crucial hour of Oswald's interrogation, no one who was not connected with the Dallas police force was present. We have only Fritz's word about what was said then.

Perhaps even more astonishing is the second revelation contained in that paragraph. What it says is that Oswald, arrested forcibly in a movie theater after pulling a gun and striking a policeman, was brought to police headquarters as a suspect in the murder of a policeman and the assassination of the President, held for some two hours, questioned by the chief of the homicide bureau, transported around the building, *and never searched!*

"While waiting outside the lineup room (some time after 4:05 p.m.) Oswald was searched and five cartridges and other items were removed from his pockets," the Report says.

Suppose Oswald had been carrying another gun, or a knife, or a bottle of nitroglycerine, or a cyanide capsule? Carelessness again? Or were the police of Dallas hoping that Oswald would do something during those first desperate hours after his arrest that would give them an excuse for shooting him themselves?

The Commission's efforts to dispel suspicion of a conspiracy come under serious question on a number of other scores as well.

Above all, there is the question of the number and direction of the shots that killed Kennedy and wounded Connally. This question will be examined in more detail later. For now, it is enough to say that the Commission's determination that three bullets were fired and that all came from the book depository *is far from conclusive*, as are the Commission's findings that all of President Kennedy's wounds originated from behind and that Connally was hit by a bullet which had first hit the President.

Many witnesses, including some never called to testify

by the Commission, were certain that the first shot came from an area either on or near the Triple Underpass, which lay directly ahead of the Presidential motorcade. If these witnesses are correct, and the Commission gives us no real reason to doubt them, then Oswald was only one of at least two persons shooting at the President.

In addition, doctors at Parkland Hospital, who were the only medical men to see the President's wounds in their original state, decided at the time that the puncture in President Kennedy's throat was a wound of entry; in other words, that the President had been shot in the throat by someone standing in front of him.

In order to grasp the implausibility of the Commission's contention that Oswald was alone and unaided at any point either in the assassination itself or his subsequent flight, let us now take the story step by step, checking each element to see whether the evidence offered by the Commission supports or denies the existence of accomplices.

As the Presidential motorcade turned the corner from Houston Street into Elm Street, Oswald, crouching at the sixth-floor window, drew a bead on the President through a telescopic sight. A tree obstructed his view of Kennedy for a few seconds, then the car moved into the open and headed down Elm Street toward the Triple Underpass.

What happened next, according to the Warren Commission's description, is this:

Oswald pulled the trigger, got off a shot at the President, drew the bolt on his rifle, restored the bolt, aimed again, fired a second bullet, then went through the entire loading, aiming and firing procedure a third time.

According to the Commission, one bullet missed, two hit. One entered President Kennedy's back and exited through his neck, the other hit him in the back of the head, blowing off part of his skull.

If the second shot missed, the entire sequence had to be completed in less than 5.6 seconds. If the first or third shot missed, the total time involved for the shooting must have been less than 8 seconds, the Commission tells us.

In other words, three shots were fired in something under 8 seconds by a poor marksman using a cheap bolt-action Italian rifle. And two hit their mark with deadly accuracy.

Many gun experts say this is improbable if not downright impossible.

They say—and the Commission's tests proved—that an extraordinary marksman would find it difficult to fire with such accuracy in so short a time span using the Carcano rifle Oswald fired. For Oswald, who made low scores on his two rifle tests in the Marine Corps, such a performance would be unlikely indeed. And this is supposedly the same man who missed General Walker, a fixed and silhouetted target, from point-blank range.

If Oswald fired three shots, which appears to be the case judging from the discovery of three spent cartridges on the floor near the book depository window, and hit once, the story would be far more believable. This version would require a fourth shot to have been fired from the front of the motorcade by an accomplice. This shot would be the one that hit the President in the neck.

The next development also raises the spectre of an accomplice. A policeman, Deputy Constable Seymour Weitzman, found a rifle between some cartons near the back stairway of the sixth floor of the book depository. He identified the rifle as a 7.65 mm. Mauser, a German-made gun. For almost 24 hours, the rifle believed to be the assassination weapon was described by police officials and by District Attorney Henry Wade—a former FBI agent—as a German Mauser. Only the next day did the story change. At that time, police unveiled for the press a rifle which they described as the weapon used by Oswald to kill Mr. Kennedy. But this rifle was an Italian-made 6.5 mm. Mannlicher-Carcano.

Even a casual glance at the rifle the police showed that

day revealed that it bore two legends on it. "Made Italy" and "Cal. 6.5." Although the Commission says an erroneous identification was made, it is hard to understand how a gun bearing the words "Made Italy" and "Cal. 6.5" could be mistaken for a 7.65 German Mauser. *Or were there two guns?*

Next we come to Oswald's departure from the book depository. The Commission tells us that the building was sealed at about 12:37 p.m., although it is evident that many police had reached the building before that time in response to a radio call from Chief Jesse Curry moments after the shooting. Yet Oswald managed to run down four flights of stairs, meet Patrolman Baker and Roy Truly on the second floor, talk to them, get a bottle of Coke, stroll across the lunchroom, and leave the building without being stopped.

The next episode is even more bizarre. Oswald went to his rooming house, got a gun, put on a jacket and left, according to the Commission's reconstruction of his movements. But before his departure, a curious incident occurred.

The story is told by Mrs. Earlene Roberts, the housekeeper at Oswald's rooming house at 1026 North Beckley Avenue. She said that at about 1 p.m., while Oswald was still in his room, where he remained a total of only three or four minutes before leaving, a Dallas police car drove up to the rooming house.

"Right direct in front of that door, there was a police car stopped and honked," she told the Commission. "I had worked for some policemen and sometimes they come by and tell me something their wives would want me to know, and I thought it was them, and I just glanced out and saw the number and I said, 'Oh, that's not their car,' for I knew their car."

Joseph A. Ball, the Commission assistant counsel questioning Mrs. Roberts, asked her: "Where was it parked?"

"It was parked in front of the house," she answered.

"And then they just eased on, the way it is, it was the third house off Zangs and they just went on around the corner that way."

"Did this police car stop directly in front of your house?" Ball persisted.

"Yes," Mrs. Roberts replied. "It stopped directly in front of my house and it just 'tip-tip' and that's the way Officer Alexander and Charles Burnley would do when they stopped, and I went to the door and looked and saw it wasn't their number."

"Where was Oswald when this happened?" Ball asked.

"In his room," Mrs. Roberts said.

A moment later, Ball took the testimony one step farther.

"Were there two uniformed policemen in the car?" he asked.

"Oh, yes," Mrs. Roberts replied.

"And one of the officers sounded the horn?" Ball asked.

"Just kind of a 'tit-tit'—twice," Mrs. Roberts said.

Mrs. Roberts was uncertain about the number on the police car. The Commission report says she testified at first that she thought the car was number 106, then said it was 107. She told the FBI it was car number 207.

The Commission says that "investigation has not produced any evidence that there was a police vehicle in the area of 1026 North Beckley at about 1 p.m. on Nov. 22. Squad car 207 was at the Texas School Book Depository Building, as was car 106. Squad cars 170 and 107 were sold in April, 1963, and their numbers were not reassigned until February, 1964."

This is another of those strangely bland comments one finds throughout the report. Does the Commission believe that if a police car had pulled up to Oswald's rooming house to blow its horn as a signal, its occupants would have informed the police dispatcher at headquarters of their actions? And why does the Commission assume that simply because a police car is sold, it ceases to exist and is no longer available for use? Who bought the two police cars? We are not told.

Perhaps the most dramatic example of what has since been blamed entirely on police carelessness was the shooting of Oswald by Ruby.

Once again, we can read this incident in two ways. Either it is another demonstration of monumental ineptitude, and this is the way the Warren Commission chooses to understand all of these incidents, or it was part of a scheme that reached its culmination with Oswald's death.

Again let us review the circumstances. Oswald had been in custody for just under 48 hours. On Sunday morning, the police undertook to move him from police headquarters to the county jail. Dallas police officials, cooperating fully with the press and especially with TV newsmen, announced in advance the approximate time of the transfer so that reporters and equipment could be installed on the scene.

Nevertheless, security measures were tight, according to police officials and the Warren Commission, both during and before the abortive transfer.

"Police control over the access of other than newsmen to the third floor (of Police Headquarters) was of limited but increasing effectiveness after Oswald's arrival at the police department," the Commission Report says. "Initially, no steps were taken to exclude unauthorized persons from the third floor corridor, but late Friday afternoon Assistant Chief Batchelor stationed guards at the elevators and stairways to prevent the admission of such persons. He also directed the records room in the basement to issue passes, after verification by the bureaus involved, to people who had legitimate business on the third floor. . . .

"Newsmen seeking admission to the third floor were required to identify themselves by their personal press cards. . . . .Police officers on the third floor testified that they carefully checked all persons for credentials."

At least one Secret Service man was asked for his credentials before he was admitted to the third floor.

Despite all this evidence of tight security, Jack Ruby "was present on the third floor on Friday night," the Report states.

By Sunday, the day of the transfer, the confusion in the police building had abated somewhat. On Saturday night, Police Chief Curry had told reporters: "If you are back here by 10 o'clock (the next morning), you will be back in time to observe anything you care to observe."

Sunday morning, between 2:30 and 3 a.m., the FBI and the Dallas sheriff's office received phone tips warning that a committee had been formed to kill Oswald. The tips were passed along to Chief Curry and other Dallas police officials and when Curry arrived at his office around 8:30 that morning, he discussed the plans to transfer Oswald with Sheriff Decker. Curry decided that the police would direct the transfer, rather than the sheriff's office, because "we had so much involved here, we were the ones that were investigating the case and we had the officers set up downstairs to handle it."

The Report says that Curry decided Oswald would be taken out of the building through the basement. Two Dallas police officials suggested to Captain Fritz that Oswald be moved through another exit, leaving the press corps waiting vainly in the basement. "We could be to the county jail before anyone knew what was taking place," these police officials told Fritz. But the captain said he did not think Curry would agree to the deception because he had promised that the newsmen would have an opportunity to photograph Oswald.

Secret Service agent Forrest Sorrels also urged Fritz to intervene with Curry in an attempt to have Oswald moved at an unannounced time. Fritz again rejected the idea, saying Curry "wanted to go along with the press."

Despite the tips that Oswald's life was in danger, and despite the urgings of two police officials and a Secret Service agent, Curry and Captain Fritz took Oswald out of the building by the route which, as it turned out, exposed him to Ruby.

At about 9 a.m. Sunday, police cleared the basement of all but police personnel, the report says. Guards were posted at the entrances to two ramps leading into the basement, at each of five doorways into the garage, and at a double door opening into a hallway adjacent to the jail office. A thorough search was conducted of the entire area. Fourteen policemen checked every closet and room opening off the basement garage. They looked into the air-conditioning ducts and searched the rafters. They checked the interiors and trunks of every car parked in the garage. They ordered maintenance men working in the garage to leave, locked the doors of the two passenger elevators giving access to the garage, and ordered the operator of a service elevator to take his car up to the first floor and stay there. Only after the search was completed were newsmen allowed to enter the basement. The police had firm orders from Capt. C. E. Talbert and Sgt. Patrick T. Dean to permit no one but newsmen showing authentic credentials to enter.

More than 70 policemen were present when Oswald, handcuffed to one detective on his right and flanked by another on his left, came into the basement.

Despite these precautions, Ruby managed to enter the basement and at precisely the right moment, step from the crowd with a .38 caliber revolver in his hand and fire a single fatal bullet into Oswald's abdomen.

Not one of the more than 70 policemen or the 30 or 40 newsmen who witnessed the killing was able to tell the Commission how Ruby got into the basement. Ruby himself said he entered simply by walking down one of the ramps.

The Commission accepted this story and concluded that "Ruby entered the basement unaided, probably via the Main Street ramp, and no more than 3 minutes before the shooting of Oswald."

It reached this conclusion despite some testimony to the contrary. Patrolman R. E. Vaughn, who was guarding the entrance to the Main Street ramp, swore that he checked the credentials of all unknown persons seeking to enter the basement through that access. Three occupants of a police car that drove up the ramp at exactly the moment Ruby must have entered it, if the Commission's version is correct, said they did not see Ruby.

Ruby's presence in the basement comes as no surprise. As we saw, he was on the third floor of police headquarters on Friday night, Nov. 22, and even attended a midnight press conference at which Oswald was displayed to reporters.

When District Attorney Wade mentioned during the press conference that Oswald belonged to the "Free Cuba Committee," Ruby was one of those who shouted, correcting Wade, that it was the "Fair Play Cuba Committee."

Although the Commission asserts this was Ruby's only brush with the events surrounding the assassination preceding his murder of Oswald, a highly reliable witness suggests otherwise.

Seth Kantor, a Scripps-Howard reporter who worked in Dallas before being assigned to the Scripps-Howard bureau in Washington, had known Jack Ruby casually for five years.

In the course of his work on Nov. 22, Kantor was at Parkland Hospital at 1:30 p.m. when Malcolm Kilduff, a Presidential press secretary, announced that Mr. Kennedy was dead. Kantor told the Warren Commission that he saw Jack Ruby at the hospital at that time.

Kantor is an experienced and reliable reporter. He gave a coherent account of his meeting with Ruby at the hospital. But the Commission decided that "Kantor probably did not see Ruby at Parkland Hospital in the few minutes before or after 1:30 p.m., the only time it would have been possible for Kantor to have done so."

Once again, the Commission simply discounts testimony, even from so good a source as this, if such testimony does not fit its conception of the events that took place.

Even after Oswald's death, the violence linked to the assassination did not entirely subside. Warren Reynolds, an automobile dealer who was one of the witnesses to Oswald's flight after the Tippit shooting, was closing his office for the night in January, 1964, when a man lurking behind a filing cabinet shot him in the head with a .22 caliber rifle. Reynolds was severely wounded, but recovered.

After the shooting, a man named Darrell Wayne Garner was picked up by the Dallas police as Reynolds' suspected assailant, but he was quickly released because of an alibi provided by Betty McDonald, who was also known as Nancy Jane Mooney. A few weeks later, Miss McDonald was arrested and charged with disturbing the peace after having a fight with her roommate. While in a cell at the Dallas city jail, which is in the police headquarters building, Miss McDonald allegedly hanged herself.

The Commission dismisses Miss McDonald's death and the shooting of Reynolds as unrelated to the assassination of President Kennedy or the murder of Officer Tippit. Another case of remarkable coincidence, it finds.

In summary, let us run down all the major elements of the case which suggest the possibility that conspiracy was involved in the assassination of President Kennedy or the shooting of Lee Oswald:

1—There is considerable doubt about the number of shots fired and the direction of at least one of the shots.

2—There is medical testimony that the bullet entered President Kennedy's neck *from the front!* This would have meant a second gunman.

3—There is an element of confusion about whether two guns, rather than one, were found after the assassination.

4—Oswald managed to leave the book depository despite the presence of a large number of policemen in the area.

5—A police car apparently pulled up to Oswald's rooming house while he was there after the assassination and signaled with its horn.

6—Ruby managed to enter the tightly guarded Dallas Police Headquarters building unseen and to shoot Oswald in the presence of more than 70 police-men.

7—Despite tips that an attempt would be made to kill Oswald, and despite warnings from two police officials and a Secret Service agent, Police Chief Curry and Homicide Bureau Chief Fritz moved Oswald via an exposed and hazardous route.

8—Two months after the assassination, one of the witnesses in the case was shot and seriously wounded. A girl instrumental in clearing his suspected assailant hanged herself in a Dallas jail cell.

Individually, almost any one of these items would warrant an investigation of tenacious intensity before the suspicion of a conspiracy was abandoned. Collect-ively, they suggest a pattern that the Commission did not recognize or acknowledge.

Laid in the context of Dallas, a city torn by hatred, and superimposed upon the background of intense politi-cal ferment surrounding President Kennedy's visit there, they raise grave doubt about the Commission's declara-tion that, despite an exhaustive investigation, it "found no evidence that either Lee Harvey Oswald or Jack Ruby was part of any conspiracy, domestic or foreign..."

Chapter Four

How Was It Possible?

To many persons in the United States and abroad, the assassination of President Kennedy seemed inconceivable. How was it possible, they asked as much in bewilderment as in anger, for the young and vigorous chief of a civilized nation to be shot down on the streets of a large city while his elaborate security shield stood helpless to protect him?

The Warren Commission and even one or two of its critics offer an answer: They say the murder of John Kennedy resulted from a gigantic chain of coincidences of Homeric proportions that led inexorably to the death of the President and the slaying of his assassin.

It is as though the Fates had drawn the strands of John F. Kennedy's life toward a single point on a Dallas street corner where a man, similarly drawn by fate and beset as well by the Furies, waited with a loaded rifle.

The Greeks of Athens' Golden Age described the world and some of its more puzzling phenomena in these terms. The Greeks were a sophisticated people who knew that it was necessary at times to couch their explanations of momentous political events in cautious language.

But they were not fools. They understood that rational, often painful, explanations lurked below the symbolism and poetry of the Homeric epic.

Nor should we be fools either. The Warren Report, as

Dwight Macdonald has noted, is our American-style Iliad. In place of poetry and grandeur, we have been given the grinding dullness of legalistic language and the purported comfort of an abundance of information, much of it irrelevant and gratuitous.

Just as the Greeks knew enough to approach their epics with something less than literal acceptance, so too should we examine the Warren Report with the realization that what Macdonald calls "the lawyer's drone, the clotted chunks of expert testimony, the turgidities of officialese, the bureaucrats' smooth-worn evasions" may obfuscate the truth far more efficiently than the dactylic rhythms and poetic euphemisms of a Homeric epic.

We can explain almost any series of events as being related only by coincidence. Until we perceive more meaningful relationships, we can find comfort in believing that an awesome national tragedy like the Kennedy assassination, filled as it is with inconsistent and seemingly irreconcilable elements, adds up simply to a series of coincidences. There is a danger in accepting such an explanation, however, for it discourages a search for relationships which may in fact exist.

Acceptance of coincidence lies at the very heart of the Warren Commission's analysis of the assassination. From start to finish, the Commission builds its edifice on a foundation of gratuitous events, each related to the other only by the flimsy bond of coincidence. Such a view grows directly out of the Commission's conclusion that Oswald and Ruby each acted alone. This being so, the Commission reasons, most of the events that preceded and followed the assassination must be seen as coincidental. To establish any other, firmer relationship between them—to see any pattern whatever—is to abandon the concept of two irrational killers, each pursuing his objective in a motivational vacuum.

Louis Nizer, the lawyer and one of the Warren Commission's strongest defenders, spells out the coincidental analysis as well as anyone who has written about the assassination.

"Most often," he says with the confidence of an attorney addressing a jury, "a tragedy of immense proportions is the result of a series of coincidences, each extremely remote, occurring at the same time."

His illustrations, however, are not so compelling as his assertions.

"When a plane inexplicably explodes in mid-air and all perish, we find it difficult to accept the theory of spontaneous occurrence of numerous coincidences, and so we rush to suspicious theories of Russian sabotage or privately planted bombs," he says.

In fact, Nizer contends, several plane crashes have been caused by nothing more sinister than a series of coincidental misplays in the cockpit. This, Nizer assures us, proves that coincidences do govern the fate of man at times.

But at times they don't. At least two major air crashes in recent years definitely were caused by explosives placed aboard the aircraft.

Coincidences occur—but so do bomb plots. To insist that coincidences cause tragedies is no more convincing than to contend that bomb plots cause them. We cannot rely on either assertion as evidence of how President Kennedy died.

But Nizer does just that. "One can see from the Warren Commission Report," he says, "that a series of coincidences, not likely to occur again in a thousand years, constitutes the true explanation."

History, even contemporary history, constantly teaches us something about ourselves. Let us look briefly at a 10-day period in February, 1965, to see if something can be learned.

During those incredible 10 days, two remarkable events occurred.

The first was the arrest of three men and a woman who had planned to blow up the Washington Monument, the Statue of Liberty and the Liberty Bell in Philadelphia. The plot was nipped before it could bloom by solid police investigation and skillful infiltration. Coincidence had no role either in the plot or in its frustration.

Nor did coincidence play a part in the second. On a chill Sunday night, Malcolm X, the black nationalist apostate of Muslim prophet Elijah Muhammad, was addressing a meeting of 400 followers in a Manhattan ballroom. Suddenly, there was a diversionary commotion in the rear of the small hall. Heads turned to see what was going on, and in that instant, two or three men leaped to their feet and shot Malcolm with an assortment of pistols and a shotgun. Malcolm fell dead, the victim of a carefully plotted assassination.

Although less obvious, the murder of NAACP worker Medgar Evers by a sniper also appeared to many to be the result of a conspiracy. Certainly, it was a killing motivated by political hatred.

Nizer cites plane crashes to demonstrate that coincidence can play a role in the fate of man. More germane, perhaps, are these political murders which suggest that conspiracy and planned violence have become a way of life in the United States and that we have become a nation given to resolving some of our problems by plot and assassination.

The reactions of the American people, and especially of the news media which speak largely for and to the nation's establishment, were interesting in this connection immediately after the Kennedy assassination.

Even before the creation of the Warren Commission on Nov. 29, 1963, and long before its work was completed some 10 months later, a confidence was voiced by many that conspiracy had played no part in the Presidential murder. The reasoning went this way: Conspiratorial assassination is not part of the American tradition; such things happen in France, in Italy, in Germany and in Latin America. But not in the United States.

Elaborate efforts were made to show that previous Presidential assassins had all been mad and had acted alone—a contention by the way that is patently incorrect in the case of the assassination of Lincoln.

Granting that conspiratorial assassination had not been a characteristic of the American tradition up to the mid-20th Century, does this mean that (1) conspiracy thus is automatically excluded from any assassination, or (2) that the tradition cannot undergo change? Obviously, the answer to both questions must be negative.

Dramatic changes were taking place in the American society at the time of President Kennedy's death. They continue to occur up to this day. Sadly, the events of the past few years—the murders of several civil rights workers, Medgar Evers, the assassination of President John F. Kennedy, and Malcolm X—suggest not that political and conspiratorial assassination is alien to the United States but that it has become a firmly rooted American social mechanism. Difficult as it is for Americans to accept, it is probable that more major political assassinations have occurred in the United States during the mid-1960s than have occurred in any other country of the world.

Regardless of whether one subscribes to the theory that Mr. Kennedy's assassination and the murder of Oswald simply were the results of a series of coincidences "not likely to occur again in a thousand years," or whether one leans to the belief that a relationship of some kind exists between the myriad pieces in the puzzle, a question is implied in the Warren Report which the Commission explored from a dozen different vantages without answering adequately: How was the assassination possible?

And concomitant to this question are others: Was the assassination possible if the Commission's description of it is accepted in toto? Could the President and Oswald have been killed in precisely the way the Commission says they were?

Often, what is seen as coincidence can be seen as well as inconsistency. In the Warren Commission Report, we are told, for example, that Lee Harvey Oswald performed an unusual feat of marksmanship in killing President Kennedy. We are also told that Oswald tried to kill General Walker, a sitting target, a few months earlier, and missed.

Let us examine this situation, for it may give us a clue to the type of coincidence the Warren Commission expects us to accept.

On the evening of April 10, 1963, the Commission says, General Walker was sitting at his desk working on his income-tax forms. Most of the lights were on in his house and the window shades were up. From Walker's description of his position—his back framed by a brightly lighted window—it is evident that he was an ideal target.

At about 9 p.m., a shot shattered the stillness of the Dallas street on which Walker lived. The bullet crashed through the window, whizzed above Walker's head, and smashed through a wall.

Oswald got home late that night. He had left a note for his wife telling her what to do if he were arrested, and she had found it while he was out. "I couldn't understand at all what can he be arrested for," Marina told the Commission. "When he came back, I asked him what had happened. He was very pale. I don't remember the exact time, but it was very late. And he told me not to ask him any questions. He only told me that he had shot at General Walker."

Marina said she decided not to ask her husband any more about the incident that night. But in the morning, she said, she began to question him further about the Walker shooting.

"He said that this was a very bad man," she testified. "That he was a fascist, that he was the leader of a fascist organization, and when I said that even though all of that might be true, just the same he had no right to take his life, he said if someone had killed Hitler in time, it would have saved many lives."

Notice that according to Marina's account Oswald did two things that were significant clues to his behavior: He told her he had attempted to shoot Walker as soon as he got home; and he later gave her a clear explanation of his motive. As we have seen already, he did neither of these things after his arrest as the assassin of President Kennedy. We shall probably never know why not.

There were no eyewitnesses to the attempted shooting of Walker, according to the Commission's report, although a 14-year-old boy told police he saw two men drive away from the scene in separate cars right after the shot was fired.

Two nights before the assassination attempt, Walker had reported to the police that a friend had seen "two men around the house peeking in windows." And immediately after the shooting, Walker reported seeing a car pulling out of a church alley next door to his house. "This car would have been at the right time for anybody that was making a getaway," Walker told the Commission.

Marina said Oswald escaped after shooting at Walker by running for some distance, then taking a bus. If a car was used by Walker's assailant, then either Oswald was not the assailant or he was not alone, for the Warren Commission repeatedly informs us, in disposing of testimony that depends on Oswald's presence in an automobile, that Oswald was unable to drive.

Aside from the fact that Oswald told Marina of his attempt to shoot Walker and gave a reason for his action, there is another inconsistency between the Walker shooting and the Kennedy assassination: In the Walker shooting, Oswald missed.

Surprise at Oswald's ineptitude in the Walker shooting would not be difficult to understand. A man trained by the Marine Corps to handle a rifle would not be expected to miss a sitting target in a fully lighted room at close range. Such a miss would be strong evidence indeed of poor marksmanship.

Yet eight months later, Oswald purportedly picked off a moving target at much greater range with two out of three quick shots.

The Commission put together a mass of evidence to show that a good marksman could fire the 6.5 mm. Carcano rifle rapidly and accurately. Such evidence is, of course, essential to the Commission's case.

Three marksmen ranked as master, the National Rifle

Association's highest category, each fired two series of three shots at standing targets spaced 175, 240 and 265 feet from a tower. None of the marksmen took longer than 8.25 seconds to fire the three-shot series. One took as little as 4.6 seconds.

All three marksmen hit the first target every time, but four of their six shots aimed at the second target missed their mark, and one of the six shots aimed at the farthest target also missed.

The results of the test show that Oswald had to perform better than one of the three rifle masters in order to meet the firing requirements set for him by the Warren Commission's description of the assassination. And he had to do it not under tranquil test conditions, but beset by the tension and apprehension of knowing the nature of his target.

Fine. Let us accept the possibility that Oswald was this good with a rifle, although there is clear evidence suggesting quite the contrary. Then if he was this good— better than one master—how did he miss a sitting target at close range with all the time he could need to aim and fire?

No test was made to determine how the masters would have done under the conditions in force during the attempt on Walker's life. But there is no doubt whatever, judging from their ability to hit the first standing target in the Commission's test, that every one of the masters could have hit Walker with every shot from now until Doomsday.

We're given a rather different picture of Oswald's marksmanship capabilities by the Marine Corps records.

The Corps has three classifications to describe marksmanship: The lowest is marksman, the second is sharpshooter, and the highest is expert.

During his period of service in the Marine Corps, Oswald took two recorded tests in marksmanship. In December 1956, he fired for a score of 212—two points above the minimum required to qualify as a sharpshooter. In 1959, Oswald scored 191, just one point above the minimum necessary to qualify as a marksman. In other words, on his last rifle test as a Marine, he was able to score only one point better than the minimum for the lowest rating there is.

Lt. Col. A. G. Folsom, Jr., the head of the Marine Corps' records branch, described the sharpshooter ranking as indicative of a "fairly good shot;" he said the low marksman rating pointed to a "rather poor shot."

So Oswald, on his last showing as a rifleman, fell into the category of "rather poor shot."

This evaluation is consistent with Oswald's performance when he attempted to shoot Walker at close range and under nearly ideal conditions. It is obviously inconsistent with his performance, as described by the Warren Commission, on Nov. 22, 1963, when the Commission says he shot with the skill of a National Rifle Association master.

Oswald, we are told, at best was a fairly good shot after intensive training in riflery and went from there to become a rather poor shot. A few years later he took a shot at a sitting target at close range and missed. Eight months after that, he had somehow transformed himself into a master rifleman who was able to fire three times in less than eight seconds at a moving target and hit at least twice, a feat that some of the best marksmen in the country could not duplicate.

The tendentiousness of some of the testimony given to the Warren Commission in this connection is appalling. Listen to a Marine Corps major explaining why Oswald's score might have fallen to the dismal level of barely qualifying as a rather poor shot.

"When he fired that 212 score, he had just completed a very intensive preliminary training period. He had the services of an experienced, highly trained coach. He had high motivation. He had presumably a good-to-excellent rifle and good ammunition," the major said.

This makes sense. But when the major tries to explain the bad score on the second test, he finds it necessary to conjure.

"We have nothing here to show under what conditions the B course (the second test) was fired. It might well have been a bad day for firing the rifle—windy, rainy, dark. There is little probability that he had a good, expert coach, and he probably didn't have as high a motivation because he was no longer in recruit training and under the care of the drill instructor. There is some probability that the rifle he was firing might not have been as good a rifle as the rifle that he was firing in his A course firing because (he) may well have carried this rifle for quite some time and it got banged around in normal usage."

Yes, it might well have been a bad day for firing the rifle, or it might well have been a poor marksman doing the firing. And was the Marine Corps rifle which Oswald carried for quite some time worse than the 23-year-old Italian rifle he used in the assassination?

The possibility exists that if Oswald could not perform with a rifle as skillfully as was necessary to carry out the assassination described by the Warren Commission, then the description is incorrect. As in so many of these situations which contain inconsistencies or depend on coincidences, it is just as reasonable and perhaps more reasonable to consider the Commission's outlines of the assassination inadequate as it is to accept the remarkable and inexplicable coincidences offered by the Commission.

Murray Kempton, the New York World-Telegram columnist, was one of many observers bothered by the marksmanship problem.

Says Kempton, writing of the Commission's use of rifle masters to check Oswald's capabilities:

"The Commission might as well have been testing the probable performance of a man who shoots in his mid-80s by testing the course with scratch golfers.

"Even so, these masters missed their target on five of their 18 shots, which was not too far above Oswald's presumed average. One master missed two of his three shots, an average worse than Oswald's. These masters shot as fast as they could. Even so, if Oswald had only 5.6 seconds to fire three shots at Kennedy, he was faster with his weapon than these masters in four cases and slower in only two.

"Still and all, when the masters had finished, Ronald Simmons, who ran their tests, told the Commission that on the basis of these results the probability of hitting the target . . . . 'was relatively high.'

"The results would indicate that the probability of Oswald's hitting the target two times out of three was, on the contrary, rather low."

Oswald's superior performance with a rifle on Nov. 22, 1963, despite his long record of poor marksmanship, is but one of the coincidences difficult to comprehend in the Warren Commission's account of the assassination. There are, as we have seen, a number of others.

There is the coincidence that caused Kennedy and Governor Connally to be struck by the same bullet. This will be examined in greater detail later, for it is crucial to the Commission's thesis that only three bullets were fired, a condition which in turn is essential to the Commission's conclusion that one man fired all the shots at the President.

There is, of course, the coincidence of Oswald's escape from the book depository, of Jack Ruby's presence at precisely the right moment in the police station during Oswald's transfer, and, as astonishing as any, there is the series of coincidences surrounding the protection of the President by the Secret Service and the FBI.

To grasp fully the extent of these coincidences, it must be remembered that Oswald did not appear—so far as the nation's security forces were concerned—out of the blue. He was know to the FBI for years. Indeed, he couldn't have done much more than he did to attract the attention of J. Edgar Hoover's super sleuths.

To begin with, after leaving the Marine Corps, Oswald defected to the Soviet Union. Not many Americans emigrate, and few indeed emigrate to the Soviet Union. Those who do invariably come to the attention of the

Central Intelligence Agency and, if they return to the United States, to the FBI, which is charged with maintaining this country's internal security.

Not only did Oswald defect, but he turned his defection into a public spectacle by staging a scene in the U.S. Embassy in Moscow which drew the attention of American correspondents in the Soviet capital. Stories were carried about Oswald's defection in many American newspapers. It took no extraordinary skill in international intelligence to discover that Oswald had attempted to renounce his American citizenship. One had only to read about it in the newspapers.

Throughout Oswald's stay in the Soviet Union, the CIA kept tabs on his activities. He was potentially valuable to the CIA as a source of information, and he was potentially dangerous to the U. S. should he decide to return to his native land as a Soviet agent.

And return he did. Not as a Soviet agent, the Warren Commission tells us, but as a disenchanted Marxist. Still, the FBI records show that Oswald was checked frequently by FBI agents from the time he returned to this country until he assassinated the President.

Not long after Oswald's homecoming, he embraced the Cuban revolution and was involved in a street fight with some anti-Castro Cubans. Oswald was arrested and he asked to see an FBI agent. Once again, the story of Oswald's escapades appeared in the newspapers and on television in New Orleans. After his release by the police, Oswald appeared on two radio broadcasts as the spokesman for the pro-Castro Fair Play For Cuba Committee.

Each of these incidents was duly observed and recorded by the ever-watchful FBI. But the FBI said nothing about them to the Secret Service, which is charged with protecting the President, and the Secret Service apparently did not read the newspapers, for its Protective Research Section files—which the Warren Commission was told contain a million names—did not have a single listing for Lee Harvey Oswald, defector to the Soviet Union, avowed Marxist, disciple of Castro.

So ineffective was the system of Presidential protection employed by the Secret Service at the time of the assassination that, the Commission discovered, not one name was contained in its special file for the Dallas-Fort Worth area, despite the fact, as the Commission notes, that Adlai E. Stevenson had been "abused by pickets in Dallas less than a month before."

(Interestingly, Robert I. Bouck, the head of the Secret Service's Protective Research Section, told the Commission that the names of two persons, who were considered dangerous to the President's safety, showed up in the special file for the Houston area, where President Kennedy had made an earlier stop on his swing through Texas. One was a woman with a history of mental illness. The other was a deputy sheriff.)

The PRS and its elaborate system of geographic files clearly failed in its primary function: To protect the President from harm. This seems to be a clear case of negligence.

So does the FBI's failure to inform the Secret Service of Oswald's actions and whereabout during the weeks before the assassination.

The FBI knew on Nov. 1, 1963, that Lee Oswald was working at the Texas School Book Depository. FBI agent James Hosty learned of this from Mrs. Ruth Paine when he interviewed her that day.

"She said that Lee Oswald was living somewhere in Dallas. She didn't know where. She said it was in the Oak Cliff area, but she didn't have the address," Hosty told the Commission.

"I asked her if she knew where he worked. After a moment's hesitation, she told me that he worked at the Texas School Book Depository near the downtown area of Dallas. She didn't have the exact address, and it is my recollection that we went to the phone book and looked it up, found it to be 411 Elm Street."

On Nov. 4, Hosty said, he telephoned the Texas School Book Depository and confirmed the fact that Oswald was working there. His attempt to learn Oswald's Dallas address from officials at the book depository failed, however, for Oswald had given them Mrs. Paine's address in Irving, Texas, as his own.

"Hosty," the Commission tells us, "did nothing further in connection with the Oswald case until after the assassination."

This despite the fact that the FBI learned a few days later that the President's motorcade would follow a route on Nov. 22 that would take it right past the book depository. This despite the fact that Hosty and the rest of the FBI knew of Oswald's long history of instability, hostility toward the United States, and open support of Fidel Castro.

Hosty, as was mentioned earlier, said after the assassination that he was surprised and shocked to learn that Oswald was being held for the murder of Mr. Kennedy because he did not believe Oswald capable of this kind of violence.

Accepting this declaration, caution would seem to have dictated a course of action in the face of what was known about Oswald that would have brought him to the attention of the Secret Service as soon as the FBI realized the President would pass in front of the building in which Oswald was employed.

But the vaunted FBI did nothing. No report was submitted to the Secret Service about Oswald's presence in the building on the motorcade route, and no warning about Oswald was given to the Dallas police.

Jack Revill, chief of the Dallas Police Department's criminal intelligence section, told the Commission that he, like the Secret Service, had never heard of Lee Oswald until the afternoon of the assassination, although the FBI had a bulging file on the future assassin. Revill also raised some doubt about Hosty's declaration of surprise upon learning Oswald was suspected of the assassination.

Revill said that when he arrived at police headquarters shortly after Oswald's arrest, he met agent Hosty in the basement.

"Mr. Hosty ran over to me and he says, 'Jack'—I now recall these words— 'a Communist killed President Kennedy.'

"I said, 'What?'

"He said, 'Lee Oswald killed President Kennedy.'

"I said, 'Who is Lee Oswald?'

"He said, 'He is in our Communist file. We knew he was here in Dallas.' At that time Hosty and I started walking off, and Brian (a detective in Revill's unit) as well as I recall, sort of stayed back, and as we got onto the elevator or just prior to getting on the elevator, Mr. Hosty related that they had information that this man was capable of this, and at this I blew up at him and I said, 'Jim. . . . !' "

Chief counsel J. Lee Rankin broke in and asked: "What did he say in regard to his being capable?"

"This was it," Revill replied. "They had—'We had information that this man was capable. . . .' "

"Of what?" Rankin demanded.

"Of committing this assassination," Revill said. "This is what I understood him to say."

"I asked him why he had not told us this, and the best my recollection is that he said he couldn't. Now what he meant by that I don't know. Because in the past our relations had been such that this type of information . . . it surprised me they had not, if they had such information he had not brought it or hadn't made it available to us."

Revill's testimony is supported to an extent by V. J. Brian, the detective who was with Revill during part of his conversation with Hosty.

Brian told the Commission Hosty "came up there and he said that Lee Oswald, a Communist, killed the President, and then Revill said, 'What?' He said, Lee Oswald, a Communist, killed the President."

Hosty has insisted he never made these remarks to Revill, and he has contended that the FBI never considered Oswald capable of assassinating the President.

Someone is lying.

If Revill's story is true, it appears that the FBI intentionally concealed its knowledge about Oswald from the Dallas police and other security agencies. The most intriguing comment Hosty is alleged to have made came when he answered Revill's question about why the FBI had not reported Oswald's murderous propensities to the Dallas authorities.

". . . My recollection is that he said he couldn't," Revill said. "Now what he meant by this I don't know."

Regardless of whether the conversation ever took place as Revill reported it, there is no doubt that the FBI had enough information on Oswald to suggest that, in view of his presence in the book depository, the Secret Service should have been alerted. This the FBI did not do, and for this failure it must accept a large share of the blame for permitting the assassination to occur.

There is still another hint of a chink in the protective armor provided for President Kennedy by the Secret Service.

On the night before the President was killed, nine Secret Service agents assigned to the detail protecting him engaged in a series of actions that were unusual indeed.

The Warren Commission calls the men's behavior "a breach of discipline" and describes it this way:

The President had ended his round of activities on Nov. 21 in Fort Worth, planning to fly to Dallas the next morning. Around midnight, after President Kennedy had gone to bed, nine Secret Service agents slipped over to the Fort Worth Press Club and had a few drinks.

Some of the agents stayed at the Press Club only 30 minutes. One stayed until 2 a.m. Two of the agents returned to their hotel after leaving the Press Club. The other seven went on to a beatnik bistro known as the Cellar Coffee House. The Commission tells us that most of the agents remained there until about 3 a.m., and that one did not leave until 5 a.m., although all had to report for assignments before 8 o'clock that morning.

These men were off duty during their visit to the Press

Club and the coffee house, but Secret Service regulations expressly forbid agents assigned to a traveling Presidential detail to drink at any time.

"All members of the White House detail and special agents cooperating with them on Presidential and similar protective assignments are considered to be subject to call for official duty at any time while in travel status," the regulations say. "Therefore, the use of intoxicating liquor of any kind, including beer and wine, by members of the White House detail and special agents cooperating with them or by special agents on similar assignments, while they are in travel status, is prohibited."

The nine off-duty agents were not the only ones involved in the visit to the beatnik coffee house. Three agents on the midnight to 8 a.m. shift guarding the sleeping President dropped into the coffee house during their half-hour coffee breaks.

A Secret Service official told the Warren Commission that agents on tour with the President usually stay within the President's hotel during such breaks. He described the visits by the working agents to the Cellar Coffee House as "neither consistent nor inconsistent with their duty."

Four of the off-duty agents who were at the Press Club and the coffee house had "key responsibilities as members of the complement of the followup car in the motorcade," the Warren Commission says. "Three of the agents occupied positions on the running boards of the car, and the fourth was seated in the car."

In spite of the obvious violation of regulations, the agents who went out on the town that fateful night were not punished. The regulations provide that "violation or slight disregard" of the ban on drinking by members of a traveling White House detail "will be cause for removal from the service." But none of the agents in this case was so much as reprimanded.

James J. Rowley, chief of the Secret Service, told the Commission that under ordinary circumstances, such infractions as these men committed would have brought stern disciplinary action. Rowley explained that nothing was done because he wanted to spare the nine agents the "stigma" of blame for the President's death.

Rowley asserted that the four Secret Service men in the followup car at the time of the assassination were in good condition and did their jobs as well after drinking and getting only a few hours' sleep as they might have after no drinking and a good night's sleep.

"They performed their duties from the time they departed in the followup car from Love Field until the point of the tragedy in a most satisfactory manner," Rowley testified. "There was nothing deficient in their actions or alertness."

The Commission admits that "it is conceivable that those men who had little sleep, and who had consumed alcoholic beverages, even in limited quantities, might have been more alert in the Dallas motorcade if they had retired promptly in Fort Worth." But it accepts Rowley's assurances and comments: "However, there is no evidence that these men failed to take any action in Dallas within their power that would have averted the tragedy."

Sen. Ralph W. Yarborough, a Texas Democrat who was riding in the motorcade a short distance behind the followup car, is less certain.

In a strong statement embodied in an affidavit submitted to the Warren Commission, Yarborough said that "... all of the Secret Service men seemed to me to respond very slowly, with no more than a puzzled look" when the shooting started.

"Knowing something of the training that combat infantrymen and Marines receive," Yarborough added, "I am amazed at the lack of instantaneous response by the Secret Service when the rifle fire began."

The first shot that hit Mr. Kennedy would not have killed him. Every doctor who examined the President's body agreed on that. All said it was the second wound— the one that blew away a portion of President Kennedy's skull—that was fatal. Secret Service men are trained to respond quickly to threatening situations. Indeed, their quick response, as Yarborough suggests, is one of their best weapons. Had a Secret Service agent seen the glint of a rifle in the window of the Texas School Book Depository, as some bystanders did, or had an agent responded more quickly after the first shot was fired, John Kennedy might well be alive today.

No one will ever know what effect the night of carousing had on these four key men in the motorcade. Each of them could have been slowed down just enough that afternoon to have made a significant difference in the course of the tragedy.

The Commission displays a remarkable reluctance to explore any aspects of this bizarre episode. Why were these Secret Service men violating their regulations that night? Was this an example of their normal behavior on such trips, or was this unusual?

Rowley said the men went to the Press Club thinking they could get something to eat there but that there was no food available. He said they went to the coffee house "primarily, I think, out of curiosity, because this was some kind of beatnik place where someone gets up and recites or plays the guitar." Is beat poetry, guitar playing and a curiosity about beatniks enough to keep a Secret Service agent responsible for the President's life interested until 5 a.m.?

Unfortunately, we shall probably never know the answers to these or other questions about this nocturnal outing, for they were never asked by the Warren Commission.

Only one of the four Secret Service agents who rode the followup car after drinking at the Press Club and visiting the beatnik coffee house was called to testify before the Commission.

This witness, Clinton J. Hill, was questioned about the strange episode in which Jackie Kennedy climbed to the trunk of the Presidential limousine after her husband was shot, for he was the agent who rescued the First Lady. But he was asked nothing about his activities the night before the assassination of the President.

Among the other three men who had been out with Hill and were assigned to the followup car, none was ever asked to testify, nor were despositions taken from any one of them.

Obviously the Commission chose to listen only to the official account of this incident given by the chief of the Secret Service. The Commission did not seem to want to pursue questions about how the night on the town originated or precisely what took place during those in the Cellar Coffee House.

The Commission thus ignores an intriguing and potentially revealing facet of the assassination. It fails to determine for itself, through its own questioning of the actual participants, what effect the sleeplessness and drinking might have had on the agents in the followup car. Instead, it accepts the finding of a Secret Service official who admitted that he had given the case special consideration to avoid stigmatizing any of his men.

Chapter Five

How Many Shots Were Fired?

One of the most bewildering aspects of the Kennedy assassination is the question of how many shots really were fired during those terrifying few seconds on the afternoon of November 22, 1963.

At casual glance, this would seem to be one of the simpler problems the Warren Commission had to solve. The shots were fired in the presence of thousands of witnesses, including many who were familiar with the sounds of rifle fire. Three spent cartridge cases, a nearly whole bullet and several fragments of bullets were found after the assassination. Surely, one would think, the Commission had enough physical evidence and had located a sufficient number of witnesses to determine beyond any doubt how many shots were fired.

But this is not the case. Instead of a comprehensive and convincing answer to this crucial question, we are given contradictory statements, evasions and dubious conclusions.

The Commission tells us that "the weight of evidence indicates that there were three shots fired" at the President's car in the assassination. It bases this finding largely on two bits of evidence: The testimony of a number of witnesses that they heard three shots, and the discovery of three spent cartridges in the room at the southeast corner of the sixth floor of the book depository.

How solid is this evidence? Not very solid, as the Commission is forced to admit, at least in regard to the testimony of the witnesses.

"The consensus among the witnesses at the scene was that three shots were fired," says the Commission. "However, some heard only two shots, while others testified that they heard four and perhaps as many as five or six shots."

So the determination of the number of shots heard by the witnesses is open to question. But the Commission is more confident about the meaning of the three empty cartridge cases.

"The most convincing evidence relating to the number of shots was provided by the presence on the sixth floor of three spent cartridges which were demonstrated to have been fired by the same rifle that fired the bullets which caused the wounds," the Commission says, adding that "the preponderance of evidence, in particular the three spent cartridges, led the Commission to conclude that there were three shots fired."

This might be persuasive proof if only Oswald was firing at Mr. Kennedy. It pales if at least one other person was shooting at the President from another location, in which case the three spent cartridges could hardly be considered conclusive evidence of the number of shots fired. Indeed, even if Oswald alone was firing at the President, the spent cartridges would not tell us for certain how many shots he fired; it is possible that Oswald ejected an empty cartridge from his rifle before doing any shooting, in which case the three cartridges would account for only two shots.

But the Commission weaves its fabric to its own specifications. It insists that Oswald and no one else fired at the President. Then, since this conclusion can only remain plausible if a maximum of three shots were fired, it accepts the consensus of its witnesses and the discovery of three spent cartridges as proof that only three shots were fired.

A serious problem arises, however. At least two separate shots hit Mr. Kennedy. Of that there is no doubt. One hit him either in the back, as the Commission asserts, or in the front of the neck, as others suggest. Another hit him in the head.

Still another shot missed competely. This too is generally conceded and is substantiated by a witness, James T. Tague, who was watching the motorcade from a spot near the Triple Underpass when the shooting started and was struck on the cheek by an object—either a bullet fragment or a piece of pavement thrown into the air by an impacting bullet. Tague reported his injury to a deputy sheriff, who examined the place where Tague had been standing and found a mark on a curb that appeared to have been caused by a bullet.

That accounts for at least three shots. But an untidy loose end remains. Governor Connally was also wounded, you remember.

This would seem to make a total of at least four shots, thus creating an entirely different picture of the assassination from the one drawn by the Warren Commission. Four shots, after all, automatically mean at least two assassins, and more than one assassin means a conspiracy, which the Commission has rejected as a possibility.

The Commission solves this problem in an imaginative and skillful way. It tells us that one of the bullets must have struck President Kennedy in the back, gone through his neck, come out the front, hit Governor John Connally in the back, gone through his chest, breaking a rib on the way, come out just below his right nipple, slammed through his right wrist, breaking another bone there, and lodged in his left thigh.

Such a coincidence might have occurred. It is possible for a bullet to follow the course assigned to this one by the Warren Commission, given the proper alignment and an adequate velocity. But doubt creeps into the Commission's explanation almost at once: John Connally, his wife and a host of other witnesses all insist that Connally was hit by a separate bullet.

The Commission itself is uneasy about its description of how Connally was wounded.

"Although it is not necessary to any essential finding of the Commission to determine just which shot hit Governor Connally, there is very persuasive evidence from the experts to indicate that the same bullet which pierced the President's throat also caused Governor Connally's wounds," the Commission says.

"However," the Commission adds, "Governor Connally's testimony and certain other factors have given rise to some difference of opinion as to this probability...."

It is, incidentally, incredible that the Commission would make a statement like this. Nothing could be more necessary to the essential findings of the Commission than a determination of whether Connally was wounded by the same bullet that first struck Mr. Kennedy, or by another one. As we have seen, if Governor Connally was hit by a separate bullet, as he says he was, then a total of at least four bullets must have been fired. And if four bullets were fired, Oswald could not have fired all of them. It would have been impossible for him to get away four shots in the time allotted by the Commission after it viewed motion picture films of the assassination.

Governor Connally's testimony about what happened during the shooting was devastating to the Commission's theory of a single shot wounding both the Governor and the President. Connally, you will remember, was riding in the jump seat right in front of President Kennedy, and, as the motorcade turned into Elm Street, Connally said, "I heard what I thought was a shot.

"I instinctively turned to my right because the sound appeared to come from over my right shoulder." So I turned to look back over my right shoulder, and I saw nothing unusual except just people in the crowd, but I did not catch the President in the corner of my eye, and I was interested, because once I heard the shot in my own mind, I identified it as a rifle shot, and I immediately —the only thought that crossed my mind was that this is an assassination attempt.

"So I looked. Failing to see him, I was turning to look back over my left shoulder into the back seat, but I never got that far in my turn. I got about in the position I am in now, facing you, looking a little bit to the left of center, and then I felt like someone had hit me in the back.

"I immediately thought that this—that I had been shot. I knew it when I just looked down and I was covered with blood, and the thought immediately passed through my mind that there were either two or three people involved or more in this or someone was shooting with an automatic rifle."

Governor Connally said he heard one shot, then was hit by a shot that he did not hear, then heard another shot, and he expressed the belief that all the shots were fired within about 10 or 12 seconds.

When Arlen Specter, a Commission lawyer, asked Governor Connally which shot hit him, the tall, handsome Texan answered without hesitation: "The second one."

"And what is your reason for that conclusion, sir?" Specter asked.

"Well," Connally replied, "in my judgment, it just couldn't conceivably have been the first one because I heard the sound of the shot. In the first place, I don't know anything about the velocity of this particular bullet, but any rifle has a velocity that exceeds the speed of sound, and when I heard the sound of that first shot, that bullet had already reached where I was, or it had reached that far, and after I heard that shot, I had the time to turn to my right and start to turn to my left before I felt anything.

"It is not conceivable to me that I could have been hit by the first bullet, and then I felt the blow from something which was obviously a bullet, which I assumed was a bullet, and I never heard the second shot—didn't hear it. I didn't hear but two shots. I think I heard the first shot and the third shot."

"Do you have an idea as to why you did not hear the second shot?" Specter asked him.

"Well," Connally said, "first, again I assume the bullet was traveling faster than the sound. I was hit by the bullet prior to the time the sound reached me, and I was in either a state of shock or the impact was such that the sound didn't even register on me, but I was never conscious of hearing the second shot at all.

"Obviously, at least the major wound that I took in the shoulder through the chest couldn't have been anything but the second shot. Obviously, it couldn't have been the third, because when the third shot was fired, I was in a reclining position, and heard it, saw it, and the effects of it, rather—I didn't see it, I saw the effects of it —so it obviously could not have been the third, and couldn't have been the first, in my judgment."

Mrs. Connally's testimony gives added weight to her husband's contention that the second shot hit him. She said she heard the first shot, turned and saw President Kennedy clutching his throat.

"Then very soon there was the second shot that hit John (her husband). As the first shot was hit, and I turned to look, at the same time I recall John saying, 'Oh, no, no, no!' Then there was a second shot, and it hit John, and as he recoiled to the right, just crumpled like a wounded animal to the right, he said, 'My God, they are going to kill us all.'"

Just as damaging to the Commission's claim that a single bullet hit both Mr. Kennedy and Mr. Connally is the testimony of several doctors who examined the two men and studied their wounds.

Dr. Charles F. Gregory, a Parkland Hospital physician who attended Connally on the day of the assassination, said he believed that the bullet that hit Connally had "behaved as though it had never struck anything except him."

Dr. George T. Shires, another Parkland doctor, came to the same conclusion. Asked by Specter whether he thought it possible that one bullet went through the

President's neck, then caused all the wounds in Connally's body, Shires replied:

"I assume that it would be possible. The main thing that would make me think that this was not the case is that he remembers so distinctly hearing a shot and having turned prior to the time he was hit, and in the position he must have been—I think it's obvious that he did turn rather sharply to the right and this would make me think that it was a second shot. . . ."

Aside from insisting that he was hit by a separate bullet from any that struck President Kennedy, Governor Connally raised an interesting point in his testimony that the Warren Commission ignored as a possibility. He suggested that his chest wound might have been caused by a different bullet from the one that broke his wrist and punctured his thigh. "At least the major wound that I took in the shoulder through the chest couldn't have been anything but the second shot," Connally said, leaving open the possibility that the wrist and thigh wounds might have been caused by still another bullet.

The idea draws considerable support from two doctors who testified before the Commission. The questioning of these doctors revolved around the Commission's belief that the bullet it says struck Mr. Kennedy in the back and passed through Connally's body eventually fell from the Governor's thigh wound and was found on his stretcher at Parkland Hospital.

Dr. James J. Humes, who performed the autopsy on Kennedy on the night of Nov. 22, was asked by Commission lawyer Arlen Specter whether this nearly whole bullet "could have been the one to lodge in Governor Connally's thigh."

"I think that extremely unlikely," Dr. Humes said. "The reports (from Parkland Hospital) tell of an entrance wound on the lower midthigh of the Governor, and X-rays taken there are described as showing metallic fragments in the bone, which apparently by this report were not removed and are still present in Governor Connally's thigh. I can't conceive of where they came from this missile."

In other words, Humes does not believe that the same bullet that caused the Governor's chest wound also caused his thigh wound. Neither does Dr. Robert R. Shaw, a member of the Parkland staff.

"As far as the wounds of the chest are concerned," he told the Warren Commission, "I feel that this bullet could have inflicted those wounds. But the examination of the wrist both by X-ray and at the time of surgery showed some fragments of metal that make it difficult to believe that the same missile could have caused these two wounds."

Not one eyewitness ever volunteered the opinion to the Warren Commission that Connally was struck by the same bullet that hit Mr. Kennedy. The Commission reached this conclusion, in spite of a wealth of evidence against it, in spite of Connally's own account of what happened.

If the Commission had accepted the implications of its evidence and had concluded that Connally was wounded by a separate bullet, that would have been the end of the neat picture of the assassination as the work of one deranged man acting alone. As we have seen, if Connally was hit by a separate bullet, four or more bullets were fired, and if at least four bullets were fired, more than one man was firing.

As confusing as the Warren Commission's description of Connally's wounds may be, it is no more confusing than the Commission description of President Kennedy's wounds.

According to the Commission, you will recall, President Kennedy was shot once in the back and once in the back of the head. The first bullet, the Commission says, struck President Kennedy at a point about 5½ inches below the tip of the right mastoid process—which is the bone behind the ear—and about the same distance from the tip of the right shoulder joint. This bullet, the Commission says, cut through the President's body and exited at a point on the neck where Mr. Kennedy's tie knot was located, or just below the Adam's apple. The second bullet that hit the President entered his head from the right rear, the Commission found, and exited from the right front.

Two groups of doctors examined the President after he was shot. One group was at Parkland Hospital, in Dallas, where the President was taken right after the shooting and where he was pronounced dead. The second group of doctors examined his body at Bethesda, where the autopsy was performed.

During the autopsy, X-rays and photographs were made of the President's body and its wounds. These vital medical records were turned over to the Secret Service by the Bethesda doctors and have never been shown to the public. Not even the members of the Warren Commission have seen these invaluable records.

Instead of studying these photographs and X-rays, the Commission relied heavily on two sources of information to determine the location of the President's wounds: The testimony of the doctors who performed the autopsy, and some rough though informative drawings made by a medical illustrator who had not seen the photographs or X-rays either, but who drew the sketches at the direction of one of the Bethesda doctors.

No original notes on the autopsy survive. In an act reminiscent of Capt. J. W. Fritz's destruction of his notes on Oswald's interrogation, they were burned by the doctor who made them.

Dr. James J. Humes admitted that he destroyed the notes in a sworn statement on November 24, two days after the autopsy was completed. "I, James J. Humes, certify that I have destroyed by burning certain preliminary draft notes relating to Naval Medical School Autopsy Report A63-272 and have officially transmitted all other papers related to this report to higher authority."

Why did Dr. Humes destroy these preliminary but potentially revealing notes? No reason is given. Nor is any reason given for the Commission's apparent lack of interest in the X-rays and photographs of Mr. Kennedy's body, which would have provided incontrovertible proof of the location of the President's wounds.

Without the X-rays and photographs, we can never be certain of the precise location of the wounds. And without being certain of their exact location, we cannot be sure whether the picture of the assassination painted by the Commission is even possible, let alone probable.

The only tangible graphic rendering of the location of the wounds is found in the drawings made by the medical illustrator. What do they show?

One drawing depicts two full-length figures standing side by side, one seen from the back, the other from the front. Marked on these figures are the locations of the bullet wounds in the President's body. On close examination of the two drawings, we discover a remarkable situation: The bullet wound shown on the back of the figure is lower than the wound shown on the front. The two figures are exactly the same size and were drawn in accurate proportion if not in precise scale. Yet the wound on the back is lower than the one on the front.

If the drawing is correct, the bullet that presumably entered the President's back on a downward course turned inexplicably and exited in an upward direction. To complicate matters even more, this same bullet, according to the Warren Commission, then changed direction again and raced through Connally's body on a downward course.

In addition to the full-length drawings, the Commission was provided with drawings of the President's head and shoulders in side and rear views. These drawings show the back wound far differently than the full-length sketches. On the small drawings, the wound in the President's back has moved considerably higher, toward the nape of his neck, and the track in the side view is clearly downward.

One of these exhibits is obviously wrong. Only the X-rays and photographs can establish which. But we cannot see the X-rays and photographs to find out.

Vital to a determination of whether all the shots fired at Mr. Kennedy came from the book depository, as the Commission asserts they did, is not only the location but also the nature of the wounds.

There are two types of bullet wounds—those of entry and those of exit. Entry wounds are neat, small punctures made by bullets traveling at maximum velocity and without yaw. Exit wounds are tearing injuries caused by bullets that are wobbling and sweeping tissue ahead of them as they leave the body.

The best way of determining whether a wound was caused by an entering or exiting bullet is to study the wound itself. If it is jagged and torn, it is probably an exit wound. If it is neat and round, it is probably an entry wound.

Initially, the doctors who examined Kennedy at Parkland Hospital were convinced that the wound in the front of his neck was an entry wound. For one thing, they neglected to examine the President closely enough to discover the wound in his back at all. For another, the neck wound was small, round and free of jagged edges. It looked to the doctors and nurses attending the President like an entry wound.

If the wound was what they thought it was, it must have come from a gun aimed at the President from ahead of him, rather than from the book depository to his rear.

But the Warren Commission says that the autopsy performed at Bethesda established that this neck wound was an exit wound. The autopsy, the Commission says, showed that the small wound in the President's back was the bullet's point of entry, and that it cut through Mr. Kennedy's lower neck and exited at about the point where the knot of his tie lay.

Unfortunately, the doctors who performed the autopsy on President Kennedy at Bethesda could not make an empirical judgment about the neck wound because they never saw it. During the desperate efforts to save the President's life earlier that day, the doctors at Parkland Hospital had mutilated the wound in the President's neck. They had cut it open and enlarged it in order to insert a tracheotomy tube that was intended to help the President breathe.

"In the earlier stages of the autopsy," the Commission reveals, "the surgeons were unable to find a path into any large muscle in the back of the neck. At that time they did not know that there had been a bullet hole in the front of the President's neck when he arrived at Parkland Hospital because the tracheotomy incision had completely eliminated that evidence."

Only after talking to one of the Parkland doctors by phone early in the morning of Nov. 23—about two hours after the autopsy had been completed at 11 p.m., Nov. 22—did the Bethesda doctors learn that the tracheotomy incision had obliterated a bullet wound.

Since the doctors performing the autopsy did not know for quite a while that President Kennedy had suffered any neck wound at all, they would inevitably have had to conclude that the back wound was caused by a bullet entering rather than exiting his body. As far as these doctors knew, there was no point of exit for this bullet. One wonders to what extent this initial decision, based on erroneous information, colored the ultimate findings of the pathologists.

Without Dr. Humes' preliminary notes, we have no way of knowing how confused the pathologists were about this back wound, operating as they were under completely false premises.

We get one clue from the testimony of Secret Service agent Roy Kellerman, who was present during the autopsy.

"There were three gentlemen who were performing this autopsy," Kellerman told the Warren Commission. "A Col. Finck—during the examination of the President, from the hole that was in his shoulder, and with a probe, and we were standing right alongside of him, and he is probing inside the shoulder with his instrument, and I said, 'Colonel, where did it go?' He said, 'There are no lanes for an outlet of this entry in this man's shoulder.'"

In other words, Dr. Finck, unaware of the wound in Mr. Kennedy's neck, could find no track by which the bullet that entered the President's back could have exited from his body. This is mystifying.

Why was he not able to trace the bullet's track through the President's body and out the neck wound? Why did he not say, even without knowing of the neck wound but on the basis of a palpable track in the President's body, that this bullet must have exited through the neck? An expert pathologist—Dr. Finck is such an authority—should have been able to follow the course of the bullet and conclude that it must have exited from the area of the tracheotomy—unless of course this was not the case.

A possible explanation is provided by another Secret Service agent, Glen A. Bennett. Bennett was one of the four agents in the President's followup car who had visited the press club and the beatnik bistro during the night before the assassination. Although not listed as a witness, and apparently never called to testify by the Warren Commission, he is mysteriously quoted in one place in the report.

The Commission says Bennett heard a shot, which sounded to him like a firecracker, and "looked at the President."

"I heard another firecracker noise and saw that shot hit the President about four inches down from the right shoulder," Bennett said. "A second shot followed immediately and hit the right rear of the President's head."

Bennett's account suggests that President Kennedy might have been hit by three bullets: First in the neck by a shot fired from in front of him, then in the back by a second shot, and finally in the head by a third. Bennett had no view of the front of Mr. Kennedy's body since he was riding behind the President. *If that first shot hit President Kennedy in the neck, and the second hit him in the back, there would be no exit track from the back wound, since the bullets would have remained in Mr. Kennedy's body.*

As Vincent J. Salandria, a Philadelphia lawyer who studied the Commission's evidence on the number and direction of the shots, said in an article in Liberation magazine, "If Col. Finck was correct, if there were indeed no lanes of exit from such a wound, then that is the end of the Commission's theory that one assassin fired all the shots at the assassination site.

"Such a finding of no outlet would make the back wound a separate hit. It would make the front neck wound a separate hit. It would place one gunman in front of the President. It would add one bullet to the three shells found in the depository building, thereby making four, and thereby requiring another gunman to accomplish all the shooting in the maximum allowable time."

The waters grow even muddier when one looks at the clothes Mr. Kennedy was wearing when he was shot.

FBI agent Robert A. Frazier told the Commission about two little holes in President Kennedy's shirt and jacket which cry out against the Commission's version of the assassination.

"I found on the back of the shirt a hole, 5¾ inches below the top of the collar, and as you look at the back of the shirt 1⅛ inch to the right of the midline of the shirt . . ." Frazier said. He added that he found a similar hole in the President's jacket 5¾ inches below the top of the collar and 1¾ inches to the right of the mid-seam. The slight difference in the positioning of the two holes, Frazier explained, could be accounted for "by a portion of the collar sticking up above the coat about a half inch."

Try a little experiment yourself. Get a jacket and measure 5¾ inches from the top of the collar along the mid-seam in the back. Now move 1¾ inches to the right. That spot is precisely where Frazier said Kennedy was shot. *Now try to figure out how a bullet entering at that point could travel downward and exit from a spot just below the President's Adam's apple. As you will discover, it is an impossibility.*

The Warren Commission notes the presence of the holes in President Kennedy's shirt and jacket and their location, but makes no comment on their implicit contradiction of the Commission's assertion that the bullet entered Mr. Kennedy's back on a downward course and exited from his neck.

During the investigation, Commission lawyer Arlen Specter and Dr. Humes attempted to explain this contradiction by noting that President Kennedy was muscular and had his right hand raised, thus hiking his jacket and shirt up, when the bullet struck him. In fact, Mr. Kennedy's arm was raised only slightly, his elbow bent and his hand at about forehead level, as movies of the shooting establish. And even if both his arms had been raised high above his head, the jacket and shirt would not have risen nearly far enough to permit the bullet to penetrate the jacket where it did, move downward, and exit as the Commission says it did.

Now let us take a look at how substantially the Commission supports its contention that the wound in President Kennedy's neck is an exit wound. Since the doctors at Parkland Hospital were the only ones who saw the wound in its original state, before the tracheotomy destroyed it, what did they say about it?

Dr. Malcolm Perry is a Parkland doctor who was deeply involved in the efforts to save the life of the mortally wounded President.

"Based on the appearance of the neck wound alone," he was asked by a Commission lawyer, "could it have been either an entrance or an exit wound?"

"It could have been either," Dr. Perry replied.

Dr. Charles J. Carrico, also a member of the Parkland staff, described the neck wound as "fairly round" and free of jagged edges, and Dr. Charles R. Baxter said it was "a spherical wound," adding: "Well, the wound was, I think, compatible with a gunshot wound. It did not appear to be a jagged wound such as one would expect with a very high velocity rifle bullet. We could not determine, or did not determine at that time, whether this represented an entry or exit wound. Judging from the caliber of the rifle that we later found or became acquainted with, this would more resemble a wound of entry."

Ronald C. Jones, another Parkland doctor, went even further. Declaring that he thought the neck wound was caused by a bullet entering rather than leaving the President's body, Dr. Jones said:

"The hole was very small and relatively clean cut, as you would see in a bullet that is entering rather than exiting from a patient. If this were an exit wound, you would think that it exited at a very low velocity to produce no more damage than this had done, and if this were a missile of high velocity, you would expect more of an explosive type of exit wound, with more tissue destruction than this appeared to have on superficial examination."

If, then, this was a bullet traveling at the normal speed of rifle bullets, it was in Dr. Jones' opinion an entry wound. If for some reason this bullet was traveling at an inordinately slow speed, however, how could it possibly have continued on its purported course through Kennedy's neck, into Governor Connally's back, through his chest, through his wrist and into his thigh? Slow-moving bullets do not penetrate that far.

And still another problem arises. If the bullet that assertedly exited from President Kennedy's neck made such a clean little wound, without inflicting more tissue damage than it did, why did another bullet fired from the same gun moments later enter the back of Kennedy's head and blow off a large portion of his skull on exiting?

Not only does the Commission deprive us of the conclusive evidence about the wounds that exists in the photographs and X-rays made during the autopsy, but by a peculiar omission it deprives us of a description of the wounds that might have shed important light on them.

In Jacqueline Kennedy's testimony to the Commission, she told how the shooting started, and how she heard a voice cry, "Get to the hospital," and how President Kennedy fell into her lap mortally wounded.

At this point in her testimony, a bracketed statement appears. It says: "Reference to wounds deleted."

We are given no explanation for this censorship of testimony by the Commission. Presumably the Commission was concerned about the sensibilities of the American people. Describing the wounds was not too much for Mrs. Kennedy, but apparently the Commission decided reading her description would be too much for the American people to bear.

The Warren Commission's concern is misplaced. We do not need the Commission's solicitousness for our sensibilities. That was not the Commission's function. Its purpose was to provide us with the truth. We counted on the Warren Commission to provide us with the most complete record of the assassination that we could hope to obtain. Along with other omissions and evasions, the deletion of Mrs. Kennedy's description of her husband's injuries suggests that we did not get what we had a right to expect.

Even more alarming is the possibility that the Commission deleted this description because Mrs. Kennedy's words conflicted with the Commission's own version of what the President's wounds were like. By deleting this testimony, the Commission leaves itself vulnerable to the charge that it was intentionally hiding something.

As we have seen, the evidence to support the Commission's thesis that Governor Connally was hit by the same bullet that hit President Kennedy is seriously challenged by evidence suggesting that Connally was hit by a separate bullet. In addition, there remain many questions about whether Mr. Kennedy's back and neck wounds originated in precisely the way the Commission says they did.

That means it is altogether possible that more than three shots were fired and that at least one came from a place other than the book depository. Where might it have come from?

You will recall that when the first shot was fired at Mr. Kennedy, many people in the crowd watching the motorcade turned toward a railroad overpass that lay ahead of the President's car. Sheriff Decker, who was riding in the lead car in front of the President's, immediately ordered all available men from his department to go to the railroad yards.

Between the book depository and the railroad overpass, on the north side of Elm Street, there is a grassy knoll. Along its northern edge, extending all the way from the book depository to the railroad overpass, this knoll is lined with trees.

S. M. Holland, a signal supervisor for the Union Terminal Company, was standing on the overpass directly in front of the motorcade when the shooting erupted.

Holland said he heard a shot and saw President Kennedy clutch his throat. Then he heard another shot which he says hit Governor Connally.

"I heard a third report and I counted four shots and about the same time all this was happening," he said, "in this group of trees..."

Holland was interrupted by Samuel Stern, a Commission assistant counsel, who asked whether Holland meant the trees on the north side of Elm Street.

"These trees right along here," Holland said, pointing on a photographic exhibit to the trees on the grassy knoll.

"There was a shot, a report, I don't know whether it was a shot," Holland continued. "I can't say that. And a puff of smoke came out about six or eight feet above the ground right out from those trees. And at just about this location from where I was standing, you could see that puff of smoke, like someone had thrown a firecracker or something out and that is just the way it sounded. It wasn't as loud as the previous reports or shots .... there were definitely four shots."

Billy W. Hargis, a motorcycle policeman who was riding to the left of the President's car when the shots rang out, said he was not sure at that moment where the shots had come from. Hargis told the Commission he leaped from his motorcycle and "ran across the street looking towards the railroad overpass and I remembered seeing people scattering and running, and then I looked .... over to the Texas School Book Depository Building and no one that was standing at the base of the building was—seemed to be looking up at the building or anything like they knew where the shots were coming from. . . ."

Hargis said he ran up the incline of the grassy knoll, found nothing alarming there, and was ordered to help seal off the book depository.

Another motorcycle cop, Clyde Haygood, also was assigned to the motorcade, but was riding a bit to the rear of the President's car. He heard shots as he made the turn from Houston Street into Elm Street.

"I could see all these people laying on the ground there on Elm," he said. "Some of them were pointing back up to the railroad yard and a couple of people were headed back up that way, and I immediately tried to jump the north curb there in the 400 block." The curb was too high for Haygood's motorcycle, so he left it on the street and "ran to the railroad yard."

Mrs. Jean Hill was standing on a grassy incline directly across Elm Street from the book depository— in other words south of the building and the grassy knoll to its west. Like every other witness who commented on the question, she said she was certain Connally "wasn't hit when the first shot hit."

Mrs. Hill, a school teacher, said she thought at least some of the shots came from the grassy knoll across the street from where she was standing. And she was convinced there were more than three shots. A few hours after the assassination, she informed a Secret Service man of her belief.

"Am I a kook or what's wrong with me?" she asked the unidentified Secret Service man. "They keep saying three shots. I know I heard more. I heard from four to six shots anyway."

Mrs. Hill said the Secret Service man told her: "Mrs. Hill, we were standing at the window and we heard more shots also, but we have three wounds and we have three bullets, three shots is all that we are willing to say right now."

With Mrs. Hill at the time of the shooting was a friend of hers, Mary Moorman. Mrs. Moorman was in the same place at the same time. But she was never summoned to testify before the Warren Commission.

Nor was Charles Drehm, a Dallas carpet salesman who told the Dallas Times Herald he was about 10 feet from the President's car at the moment of the shooting. Drehm, the Times Herald said, "seemed to think the shots came from in front of or beside the President."

Nor did the Commission call O. V. Campbell, the vice president of the book depository, who was standing in front of the building with Roy Truly, the depository superintendent, at the time of the assassination. Campbell was quoted in the Dallas Morning News as saying he "ran toward a grassy knoll west of the building" because he thought the shots were coming from there.

Nor did the Commission call four women employed by the Dallas Morning News who were on the grassy knoll itself. One of the four, Mary Woodward, wrote an eyewitness account of the assassination for the Morning News. She said she and her three companions were sitting on the knoll overlooking Elm Street when they heard "a horrible, ear-shattering noise coming from behind us and a little to the right."

If the sound came from behind the four women, it couldn't have come from a gun on the sixth floor of the book depository, which was to their left. Did the Commission question Mary Woodward or any of her three companions about this "ear-shattering noise" they heard coming from behind them? It did not.

The Commission tells us that it relied upon "the consensus among the witnesses at the scene" to reach its conclusion that three shots were fired. Such a consensus, which overlooks or ignores many actual witnesses, can hardly be considered reliable.

In fact, the Commission's evidence that only three bullets were fired proves on close examination to be a lot flimsier than one would believe possible. It boils down to the three spent cartridges, the so-called consensus of witnesses and that's about all.

And the Commission's evidence in support of its contention that Governor Connally and President Kennedy were hit by a single bullet boils down to little more.

Finally, the Commission's assertion that all the shots came from the book depository faces the challenge of eyewitness testimony to the contrary.

But if more than three bullets were fired and some of the shots were fired from a place other than the book depository, why do we get no hint of an assassin at some other spot? Why was nothing seen that suggests another assassin?

First of all, it is important to remember that while a few policemen and many witnesses ran toward the railroad overpass and the grassy knoll, the attention of most policemen was focused almost instantly on the book depository. This is because while Sheriff Decker was ordering his men to the railroad yards, Police Chief Curry was dispatching his larger force to the depository. Secondly, we must not underestimate another assassin's capacity for escape. Just because Oswald was as inept as he was, we may not assume that another gunman would be equally crude.

Still, some suspicious incidents were reported to the Commission by witnesses who were far from the book depository.

Mrs. Hill, for instance, saw a man wearing a brown hat and a long coat running from the grassy knoll immediately after the assassination. She said, with some reluctance and only after admitting that her husband had chided her for making the statement earlier, that the man resembled Jack Ruby.

Nor was the Commission able to identify everyone on the railroad overpass.

Holland, the terminal company employee, told the Commissioner he was posted on the overpass to help two policemen identify those watching the motorcade from this vantage. At first, he said, there were eight terminal company employees, all known to him, on the overpass. But just before the motorcade turned into Elm Street, Holland said, "there was quite a few come up there ..."

"These were people you recognized as employees?" Samuel Stern asked him.

"Some of them," Holland said, "and some of them I did not recognize, but I think he (the policeman) was asking for credentials."

"So," Stern asked Holland, "is it fair to say that at the time the President's motorcade turned into this area, there was no one on the overpass that you didn't know either as terminal company employees or railroad employees or as policemen?"

"Wouldn't be fair to say that," Holland replied, "because there was quite a few that came up there right in the last moments."

Lee E. Bowers, Jr., another employee of the terminal company, described a still more mysterious sequence of events just prior to the assassination.

Bowers, a tower man for the terminal, said that during the 20 minutes before the shooting, three cars drove into a dead-end street known as the Elm Street Extension, which runs off Elm Street near the book depository.

Bowers said the cars came into the area although it had been closed to all traffic earlier in the day.

The first car entered the street at about 12:10 p.m., Bowers said. "The car proceeded in front of the school depository, down across two or three tracks and circled the area in front of the tower and to the west of the tower as if he was searching for a way out, or was checking the area, and then proceeded back through the only way he could, the same outlet he came into."

The car was a 1959 blue and white Oldsmobile station wagon with out-of-state license plates and a Goldwater sticker on its bumper, Bowers recalled. This car could not have belonged to the Dallas police department since it had out-of-state plates. It is highly unlikely that it belonged to the Secret Service or the FBI, which generally do not use four-year-old station wagons and which are even less likely to carry Goldwater stickers on their bumpers.

Coincidentally, Holland had noticed a station wagon parked behind a fence on the grassy knoll after the assassination. He too had been attracted to the car's bumper, which he said was muddy, as though somebody had been standing on it to try to get a better view of the motorcade over the picket fence. Holland was not asked to describe the station wagon in any more detail.

The second car Bowers saw came into the closed street a few minutes later. This one was a 1957 black Ford "with one male in it that seemed to have a mike or telephone or something that gave the appearance of that at least." Bowers said the man was holding the microphone or telephone up to his mouth with one hand, while driving with the other. He said this car cruised around the cul-de-sac for three or four minutes and left. This sounds like it might have been a police car checking the area, although police agencies normally do not use six-year-old cars.

The third car arrived three or four minutes after the second, Bowers said. It was a 1961 or 1962 Chevrolet, white but muddy, and it had similar out-of-state plates to those on the first car, Bowers said.

The Commission gives us no clue to the significance of these cars. Details like these may suggest that something was happening on the afternoon of Nov. 22, 1963, that was vastly different from what the Warren Commission confidently tells us was happening.

The Commission's inconclusive evidence about the number of shots that were fired, the doubts that linger about the direction of the shots, the flimsy basis on which the Commission decides that Governor Connally and

President Kennedy were hit by the same bullet—all compel the belief that we have gotten something less than the full story of Kennedy's assassination from the Warren Commission.

Chapter Six

Why did Oswald Kill Tippit?

Downtown Dallas on the afternoon of November 22, 1963, was like a city gone mad. Crowds surged through the streets, traffic came to a virtual standstill, and police sirens wailed a tremulous counterpoint to the anxious voices of people reciting the dozens of rumors about the President's death born that day.

But a few miles away in the Oak Cliff section of the city, where Lee Oswald lived, life went on as usual. Mrs. Julia Postal sat in her cramped box-office outside the Texas Theater selling an occasional ticket for a double feature consisting of "Cry of Battle" and "War Is Hell." At a nearby used-car lot, Warren Reynolds tried to generate a few sales on a slow day. Over on Patton Avenue near 10th Street, William Scoggins lolled in his parked taxi munching on a sandwich.

The air of normalcy was deceptive, however, for the madness that then gripped the downtown section of the city would within moments crash like a tidal wave over this quiet residential neighborhood.

The first ripples came in a radio message to Patrolman J. D. Tippit, who was patroling his usual district of Oak Cliff in police car number 10. Tippit realized something big was going on when, at 12:44 p.m., he heard a Code 3 emergency radio call ordering all available downtown squad cars to rush to Elm and Houston Streets, the site of the Texas School Book Depository.

A minute later, Tippit was instructed to move into the central Oak Cliff area. At about the same time, the police radio crackled out a general alarm for a "white male, approximately 30, slender build, height 5 foot 10 inches, weight 165 pounds" who was wanted as a suspect in the assassination of the President.

Tippit headed toward central Oak Cliff, listening to the droning voice of the police dispatcher ordering cars here and there for about 10 minutes. Then he got on his radio and informed the dispatcher that he was at Lancaster and 8th Street in the heart of the Oak Cliff section. The dispatcher told him to stand by for "any emergency that comes in."

That was the last exchange Tippit had with police headquarters so far as anyone knows. The time was 12:54 p.m.

Lee Oswald at this time was on his way from the book depository to his rooming house on North Beckley Avenue. He got there about 1 p.m., remained three or four minutes, then left.

At 1:15 p.m., the Warren Commission tells us, Tippit was cruising down 10th Street near Patton Avenue when he spotted a man "walking east along the south side of Patton." Since Patton Avenue runs north and south, and since Commission Exhibit 1968, a map of the Tippit shooting, clearly shows that the slaying occurred on 10th Street about 100 feet east of Patton Avenue, this must be another of those sloppy errors which abound in the Report. What the Commission undoubtedly meant to say was that Tippit spotted a man walking east along the south side of 10th Street. This may seem like a small error, which of course it is, but it is alarming to find so many similar mistakes in an official government document which purports to explain to us and to future generations precisely what took place on the afternoon of Nov. 22, 1963.

In any case, Tippit, we are told, pulled alongside the

man, whose "general description was similar to the one broadcast over the police radio."

Exactly what happened next is unclear. In one place, the Warren Commission says, "Tippit stopped the man and called him to his car." In another place, the Report says nothing about Tippit calling the man over, but merely notes that the man "walked over to Tippit's car, rested his arms upon the door on the right hand side of the car, and apparently exchanged words with Tippit through the window."

After concluding this conversation, Tippit got out of his car and started to walk toward its front. "As Tippit reached the left front wheel, the man pulled out a revolver and fired several shots," the Report says. "Four bullets hit Tippit and killed him instantly. The gunman started back toward Patton Avenue, ejecting the empty cartridge cases before reloading with fresh bullets."

Tippit's behavior in this fatal encounter was odd. The Commission says Tippit had been a policeman for 11 years and it quotes Police Chief Curry as saying Tippit was "a very fine, dedicated officer," which of course is the standard description of every policeman killed in the line of duty.

As an experienced cop, Tippit must have realized that a man he suspected of being the President's assassin (he must have suspected this, else why did he stop the man at all?) would be dangerous. Yet he first engaged the man in conversation, then got out of his car to confront the man, without once radioing for help or reporting to his dispatcher that he had spotted a suspect.

Oswald's manner was odd too. When he was met by Patrolman Marrion Baker in the book depository moments after the assassination, he was calm and showed no inclination to impulsive or violent action. Similarly, although fleeing for his life after killing the President, Oswald appeared unruffled by his encounter with Tippit. He walked casually over to the police car, rested his arms on the window and chatted with the policeman. It was only after the conversation, when Tippit emerged from the car, that Oswald drew his gun and fired.

The Warren Commission says at least 12 persons saw a man later identified as Lee Oswald carrying a revolver in the vicinity of the Tippit shooting. In presenting its proof that Oswald killed Tippit, it relies on three: Domingo Benavides, a truck driver who happened to be driving along 10th Street when the murder occurred; William Scoggins, the cab driver who had parked to have lunch; and Mrs. Helen Markham, a waitress.

Benavides told the Commission he was driving a pick-up truck west on 10th Street. As he crossed the intersection a block east of Patton Avenue, he said, he saw Tippit standing next to the left door of his patrol car, then heard three shots and saw the policeman fall. Benavides said he stopped his truck about 25 feet from Tippit's car, but remained inside until the gunman had run to the corner of 10th Street and Patton Avenue.

Benavides got out of his truck then and used Tippit's police radio to report that "We've had a shooting out here." The time of this call was 1:16 p.m.

Benavides found two empty shells in the bushes where he had seen the gunman throw them, and he gave these to a policeman who arrived on the scene a few minutes later.

Although Benavides was an eyewitness to the slaying of Tippit, he never identified Oswald as the slayer. Questioned by the police on the night of November 22, the truck driver said he did not think he could identify the man who shot Tippit. On the basis of this statement, the Dallas police never took him to the police station and never asked him to try to pick Oswald out of a lineup. Benavides later told the Warren Commission that a picture of Oswald he saw on television "bore a resemblance" to the man who shot Tippit.

Scoggins' cab was parked on Patton Avenue facing 10th Street. He saw Tippit's car drive slowly east on 10th, then pull up alongside a man walking on the south side of 10th Street. Scoggins saw the man, wearing a light-colored jacket, approach the police car, but his view of what happened next was obscured by some shrubbery. He then saw the policeman get out of his car, heard three or four shots, and saw the policeman fall.

As the gunman headed back toward Patton, Scoggins got out of his cab and hid behind it. Scoggins said the gunman passed within 12 feet of him and it was he who quoted the killer as saying "poor damn cop" or "poor dumb cop."

Scoggins identified Oswald the next day as the man he had seen with the gun.

These two versions—Benavides' and Scoggins'—agree in most important details. But Mrs. Helen Markham's account has some striking differences.

She was crossing 10th Street at Patton Avenue when she noticed a young man on the southeast corner of the same intersection. She watched as the man walked along 10th Street, saw the police car approach him and stop next to him, and saw the young man walk over to the car and lean inside the passenger's side.

Mrs. Markham then described how the man appeared to step back from the police car as the policeman "calmly opened the car door," slowly got out, and started walking toward the front of the car.

At that, she said, the man pulled a gun and fired.

She heard three shots, and saw Tippit fall to the ground. Terrified, Mrs. Markham put her hands over her eyes, but a moment later she peeked through her fingers and saw the gunman "fooling" with his gun. "I didn't know what he was doing," she said. "I was afraid he was fixing to kill me."

Although the Warren Commission says Tippit was killed instantly, Mrs. Markham told George and Patricia Nash, who are researchers at Columbia University's Bureau of Applied Social Research, that when she went over to the fallen policeman, he was still alive.

"I'm the one he was talking to when he died," she said. "I couldn't understand what Tippit said. I guess he wanted me to call on the car radio and get some help. I was there with Tippit when they put him on the stretcher. He was dying."

Mrs. Markham told the Nashes she stood next to the wounded policeman "hollering and screaming, trying to get help" but that nobody responded to her cries. "I would guess that it was about 20 minutes before the ambulance came—20, 25 minutes I was there alone until the ambulance came and then another five minutes until the police came."

Curiously, she never said a word about seeing Benavides making the call on Tippit's police radio at 1:16 p.m.

The Warren Commission says that Mrs. Markham's description of Tippit's killer was the one that was used by the police, who sent out a message at 1:22 p.m., describing the slayer as "about 30, 5 foot 8 inches, black hair, slender."

Mrs. Markham's account of the events is confusing. She signed an affidavit for the Dallas police on November 22 saying Tippit was shot at 1:06 p.m. If the shooting did occur at this time, Oswald couldn't have been the gunman, because it would have been impossible for him to reach the scene of the shooting by then. As the Commission points out, he could only have reached the intersection of 10th Street and Patton Avenue at 1:15 by walking briskly from his rooming house about nine-tenths of a mile away.

Mrs. Markham's testimony is equally confusing when she says she was with Tippit for about 20 minutes before anyone else arrived. Even if the shooting occurred at 1:06, Mrs. Markham could not have been there alone for 20 minutes because Dallas police records show that the description of the suspected killer that she gave to cops on the scene was broadcast to police cars throughout the city at 1:22 p.m., only 16 minutes after the earliest time of the murder.

"However," says the Commission, "even in the absence of Mrs. Markham's testimony, there is ample evidence to identify Oswald as the killer of Tippit."

That evidence consists almost entirely of further testimony from purported eyewitnesses.

Two young women who lived at 10th and Patton heard shots and screams. They ran to the door of their house, they told the Warren Commission, and saw a man brandishing a gun dart across their lawn. Later, each found an empty cartridge on the lawn where the gunman had dropped it. And that night, each of the women identified Lee Oswald as the man they saw running from the murder scene.

A block away, William A. Smith heard shots, saw a policeman fall and watched a man run from the scene. Smith told the Warren Commission he recognized television pictures of Oswald as the man he saw fleeing.

Ted Callaway, the manager of a used-car lot a block from 10th and Patton, and Sam Guinyard, who worked as a porter at the car lot, also heard shots, but they disagreed on how many. Callaway said there were five; Guinyard heard three. They ran in the direction of 10th and Patton and saw a man trotting toward them, holding a revolver in his raised right hand. When the gunman saw them, he crossed the street.

"Hey, man, what the hell is going on?" Callaway shouted to the running man. The man slowed down and said something, but Callaway could not make out what it was.

Callaway ran on to 10th and Patton and found Tippit lying in the street. Callaway said Tippit's gun lay beneath him. The used-car dealer picked up the gun, then he and Scoggins got into Scoggins' cab and tried to find the fleeing killer. But he had vanished.

Four more men, Warren Reynolds, Harold Russell, Pat Patterson and L. J. Lewis, were standing on another used-car lot a block south of the murder scene. They too saw a man running south on Patton Avenue with a revolver in his hand. All but Lewis identified Oswald as the man they saw. Lewis said he wasn't sure.

The Tippit murder would seem to have been investigated thoroughly, what with all these purported witnesses. But Columbia's George and Patricia Nash reported that it was not.

"We were able to locate at least two witnesses at the Tippit murder scene who were not questioned or even contacted by the Commission," the Nashes wrote.

One was Frank Wright, who lived in an apartment on the ground floor of a building about a half block east of the spot where Tippit was slain. Though never questioned by the Warren Commission, Wright apparently was the first person to arrive on the scene of Tippit's murder.

Wright told the Nashes he and his wife were watching television reports on the President's assassination when he heard shots. "I knew it wasn't backfire," he said firmly. "I knew it was shots."

Wright went to the door, noticed a police car parked up the street, and saw a man lying on the ground near the car. "It seems as if he had just fallen down," Wright said. "Maybe I saw him as he had just finished falling. He was on the ground, and then he turned over face down. . . . It seems to me that I saw him just as he hit the ground. I saw him turn over and he didn't move any more."

As Wright's eyes shifted from the fallen figure, he saw another man standing "right in front of the car . . . . looking toward the man on the ground."

This second man, Wright said, "stood there for a while and looked at the man on the ground, then as fast as he could, he got into his car. His car was a gray, little old coupe. It was about 1950-51 . . . . He got in that car and he drove away as quick as you could see."

At about the same time Wright came out of his house, or possibly seconds later, he said, "a woman came down from her porch" about three or four doors from the intersection of 10th and Patton, and on the same side of the street as Tippit's car.

"Just as the man in the car pulled away," Wright said, "she came toward the police car and then she stepped back. I heard her shout, 'Oh, he's been shot!', throwing up her hands. Then she went back up toward the house.

"There was no one out there except me and that woman when I got there, except for the man I described earlier. I couldn't figure out who did the shooting. I didn't see a gun on the man who was standing in front of the car. There wasn't anyone else but the man who drove away and the woman who come down from her porch. I was the first person out."

Wright said an ambulance summoned by his wife arrived soon after he reached Tippit's body. By that time, he said, about 25 people had gathered around the fallen policeman and his body had been covered with a blanket. "Then after a while, the police came up," Wright said, but when he tried to tell "two or three people what I saw, they didn't pay any attention."

Wright added:

"I've seen what came out on television and in the papers but I know that's not what happened. I know a man drove off in a gray car. Nothing in the world's going to change my opinion. I saw that man drive off in a gray coupe just as clear as I was born. I know what I saw. They can say all they want about a fellow running away, but I can't accept this because I saw a fellow get in a car and drive away."

It's entirely possible that Wright was mistaken or, as the Nashes suggest, there is some plausible explanation for the mysterious figure driving away from the scene in a gray coupe.

What is difficult to understand is how the Warren Commission, which purported to be conducting one of the most thorough investigations in history, could have overlooked such a potentially important eyewitness as Frank Wright.

As the Nashes also note, it becomes even more incredible when you realize that it was Wright's wife who telephoned the police to report the shooting.

"I heard three shots," she told the Nashes. "From my window I got a clear view of a man lying there on the street. He was there in the next block. I could see there was a man lying in the street. I didn't wait a minute. I ran to the telephone. I didn't look in the book or anything. I ran to the telephone, picked it up and dialed 'O.' I said, 'Call the police, a man's been shot!' After that I went outside to join my husband. It wasn't but a minute till the ambulance got there."

When she made that call, Mrs. Wright said, the operator took her address and notified the police, who pushed a hot-line button that connected them instantly with an ambulance service.

It is as difficult to understand how the Warren Commission failed to question Mrs. Wright as it is to fathom how they neglected to talk to her husband. But, as Dwight Macdonald notes, the testimany that the Wrights would have provided, had they been summoned to testify before the Warren Commission, obviously did not fit the Commission's reconstruction of what happened on 10th Street and Patton Avenue that afternoon.

The Commission's neglect of its responsibility to question every potentially informative witness goes much further. When Mrs. Wright called for help, the message was relayed to the Dudley M. Hughes Funeral Home, which handles ambulance calls for that section of Dallas. Dudley M. Hughes, Jr. got the word from the police that there had been a shooting at 501 East 10th St., which is the Wright's address, at 1:18 p.m. He instructed Clayton Butler, an ambulance driver, and Eddie Kinsley, his assistant, to answer the call.

They got into the ambulance, sounded their siren and sped the two short blocks to the scene. They arrived there about 60 seconds later, Butler said, or about three minutes after the shooting.

This is sharply different from Mrs. Markham's account, which had the ambulance reaching the scene some 20 minutes after the shooting.

Yet neither Butler, nor his assistant, nor Dudley M. Hughes, Jr., was ever questioned by the Warren Commission. Like the Wrights, they had important testimony to give, but they were never heard.

If Wright and the ambulance drivers are accurate in their recollection, two things are obvious: Mrs. Markham's story of what took place at the scene of the shooting between Tippit and Oswald is inaccurate and, since she is the only actual eyewitness to all the events that preceded the shooting, we shall never really know what happened on that quiet Dallas street.

The Nashes shed some light on another example of apparent reluctance by the Commission to talk to witnesses whose testimony would not fit its formula.

In its section on speculations and rumors, the Commission Report says:

"Speculation.—Another witness to the slaying of Patrolman Tippit, an unidentified woman, was interviewed by the FBI but was never called as a witness by the President's Commission on the Assassination of President Kennedy. This witness is alleged to have stated that she saw two men involved in the shooting and that they ran off in opposite directions afterward."

"Commission finding.—The only woman among the witnesses to the slaying of Tippit known to the Commission is Helen Markham. The FBI never interviewed any other woman who claimed to have seen the shooting and never received any information concerning the existence of such a witness. Two women, Barbara Jeanette Davis and Virginia Davis, saw the killer immediately after the shooting as he crossed the lawn at the corner of Patton Ave. and 10th Street, but they did not witness the shooting itself. They were both interviewed by the FBI and appeared before the Commission. The Commission has no evidence that there was any witness to the slaying other than those identified in chapter IV."

Yet such a woman exists. Her name is Acquilla Clemmons. In her account, two men were standing near the police car facing Tippit just before the shooting.

Mrs. Clemmons says the FBI spoke to her, but decided not to take a statement from her because she is diabetic and in poor physical condition. Whether the FBI spoke to her or not, she is known to exist, and it is remarkable indeed that the Commission, which conducted such a complete investigation of the Tippit shooting, did not find her, if for no other purpose than to knock down her story.

Just as one wonders why these witnesses—the Wrights, Mrs. Clemmons, the ambulance driver and his assistant— were not called to testify by the Warren Commission, one also wonders why a curious coincidence, to hearken back to Nizer's word, is never noted by the Commission in describing the murder of Tippit.

The slaying took place on 10th Street and Patton Avenue and was allegedly committed by Oswald after he had killed Mr. Kennedy and stopped briefly at his room on North Beckley Avenue. Where was Oswald going when he ran into Tippit?

Presumably to prevent our suspicions from being un- duly aroused, the Report does not mention that the murder of Tippit occurred just two blocks from Jack Ruby's home on Marsalis Street.

Certainly, this coincidence gives us the right to ask whether Oswald indeed was on his way to Jack Ruby's apartment when he encountered Tippit. The Commis- sion does not explore this possibility at all.

The Warren Commission's account of Oswald's arrest about 35 minutes after the Tippit murder also contains some strange omissions.

After leaving the scene of the Tippit shooting, the Commission tells us, Oswald was seen running west on Jefferson Boulevard. Johnny Calvin Brewer, the manager of a shoe store a few doors from the Texas Theater, which is on Jefferson about eight blocks from the spot where Tippit was shot, said he heard police sirens, looked up from his work and saw a man standing in the door- way of his store.

"He was a little man, about 5 foot 9 inches, and weighed about 150 pounds is all," Brewer said.

Brewer said that when the police sirens grew fainter,

the man "looked over his shoulder, turned around and walked up West Jefferson towards the theater."

"Why did you happen to watch this particular man?" a Commission lawyer asked Brewer.

"He just looked funny to me," Brewer said. "Well, in the first place, I had seen him some place before, I think he had been in my store before. And when you wait on somebody, you recognize them, and he just seemed funny. His hair was sort of messed up and he looked like he had been running, and he looked scared, and he looked funny."

Brewer said he followed Oswald and saw him slip into the theater without buying a ticket. "He just turned and walked right straight in," Brewer said.

Mrs. Julia Postal, the cashier at the theater, also saw the man duck inside without buying a ticket. When Brewer arrived, she told him to go into the theater and find the man, then she called the police.

While Brewer and an usher, Warren H. Burroughs, were looking for the man inside the theater, the police issued an alarm recorded at 1:45 p.m. It said: "Have information a suspect just went in the Texas Theater on West Jefferson."

At least 15 policemen arrived in minutes. Detectives ordered the houselights turned up and began a search of the theater's balcony and main floor. The Warren Commission says about six or seven people were sitting in the balcony, and about the same number were on the main floor—a total of 12 or 14 people.

Patrolman M. N. McDonald entered the theater from the rear. He was met by Brewer, who pointed out the man who had walked into the theater without paying. The man, later identified as Oswald, was sitting in the rear of the main floor of the theater near the right center aisle, the report says.

Now something peculiar occurred. Although Brewer and McDonald had been standing on the stage and Brewer had pointed directly at Oswald, McDonald did not rush directly up to the suspect and arrest him. This would seem to have been a natural action for the policeman under the circumstances, but it is not what he did.

Instead, the Report says, McDonald "first searched two men in the center of the main floor, about 10 rows from the front."

McDonald was asked by a Commission lawyer why he frisked the two men before turning to Oswald.

"I wanted to make sure that I didn't pass anything or miss anybody," McDonald said. "I wanted to make sure I didn't overlook anybody or anything."

But why those two men out of all the people in the theater? What was there about those men that made McDonald feel he might be missing something or overlooking somebody by failing to search them? We do not know, because the Warren Commission did not ask McDonald these questions.

After searching the two men, McDonald walked over to Oswald, who all this time had remained quietly in his seat watching the police move through the theater, and ordered him to get to his feet.

"He rose immediately," McDonald said, "bringing up both hands. He got this hand about shoulder high, his left hand shoulder high, and he got his right hand about breast high. He said, 'Well, it is all over now.'

"As he said this, I put my left hand on his waist and then his hand went to his waist. And this hand struck me between the eyes on the bridge of the nose."

"Did he cock his fist?" McDonald was asked by a Commission lawyer.

"Yes, sir: Knocking my cap off," McDonald said.

McDonald responded by hitting Oswald on the face. At this point, McDonald said, he felt Oswald drawing his gun and they struggled for it. "Whenever I hit him, we both fell into the seats," McDonald recalled. "While we were struggling around there, with this hand on the gun. . . ."

"Your left hand?" the Commission counsel asked.

"Yes, sir," McDonald replied. "Somehow I managed to get this hand in the action also."

"Your right hand?" the lawyer asked.

"Yes, sir," McDonald said. "Now, as we fell into the seats, I called out, 'I have got him' and Officer T. A. Hutson, he came to the row behind us and grabbed Oswald around the neck. And then Officer C. T. Walker came into the row that we were in and grabbed his left arm. And Officer Ray Hawkins came to the row in front of us and grabbed him from the front. By the time all three of these officers had got there, I had gotten my right hand on the butt of the pistol and jerked it free."

Under further questioning, McDonald said that during the scuffle, Oswald apparently had attempted to shoot him because the hammer of Oswald's gun "had grazed across my hand . . . . and I heard a snap."

McDonald also said that when he jerked the pistol from Oswald's hand, "it grazed me across the cheek here," scratching him from "just above the eye to just above the lip."

McDonald remembered Oswald's comment, "Well, it is all over now," but was unable to recall anything else Oswald said during the arrest.

"He was cursing a little bit and hollering police brutality," McDonald said, but added, "I couldn't recall the exact words. It was just mixed up words, people hollering and screaming when they get arrested."

"What did he say about police brutality?" the counsel asked McDonald.

"One thing," McDonald replied, " 'Don't hit me any more.' I remember that."

"Did somebody hit him?" the lawyer asked.

"Yes, sir, I guess they did," McDonald said.

"Who hit him?" the lawyer asked. "Do you know?"

"No sir; I don't, other than myself."

Although there were at least 12 and possibly 14 persons in the theater, the houselights were up and the entire arrest was staged in an open area visible to everyone present, only three witnesses to the arrest other than policemen were called to testify before the Warren Commission. One was Johny Calvin Brewer, the shoe store manager. The other two were patrons of the theater.

The Commission identifies these two patrons as George Applin, Jr., and John Gibson.

Applin told the Commission he saw Oswald struggling with four or five policemen before being subdued. But he added something to the description that no policeman mentioned. He said he saw one cop grab a shotgun by the muzzle and slam Oswald in the back with the butt end of the weapon.

Gibson also reported something not recounted by the cops. He said that while the police were fighting to subdue Oswald, one of them shouted: "Kill the President, will you."

"It is unlikely," the Report states, "that any of the police officers referred to Oswald as a suspect in the assassination. While the police radio had noted the similarity in the description of the two suspects (in the Tippit murder and the President's assassination), the arresting officers were pursuing Oswald for the murder of Tippit."

Or were they? The police radio, which every policeman in that theater unquestionably had heard, already had "noted the similarity in the descriptions of the two suspects," as the Report tells us. It seems entirely possible that one or more of the policemen in the theater had concluded that Oswald was guilty not only of the Tippit murder, but also of the assassination of the President.

No effort was made by the Warren Commission, at least on the record, to confirm the accounts of the events in the theater provided by the police and the two patrons questioned by the Commission. Nowhere are we told why only two of the 12 or 14 people in the theater were asked to testify, how they were selected to appear or why the other 10 or 12 were rejected.

Clearly, the investigations of the Tippit murder and

Oswald's arrest reinforce the impression that the Warren Commission did something less than a thorough job.

Several potentially revealing witnesses were not offerred the chance to report what they knew about the murder of Tippit. Other witnesses were not called upon to present their versions of Oswald's arrest.

These are important omissions which leave the record incomplete. Historians of the future will wonder, just as we wonder now, why these witnesses were not heard.

Chapter Seven

What Happened to Jackie?

The tragedy enacted on the streets of Dallas on November 22, 1963, touched the American people more profoundly than any single event in contemporary history. It touched us, perhaps, more deeply than many realized.

In the first full flush of grief, the nation wept as if each American had lost a loved one. The reaction, for a time at least, was awesomely real and personal, despite our long conditioning to the depersonalized and superficial emotions of television and the motivational trickery of Madison Avenue, and it bound us together as a nation in common bereavement.

This was partly because the assassination was not only a historical event of momentous magnitude. It was also a gripping national drama, a vast morality play pitting the forces of good against the forces of evil, and we were its audience and its beneficiaries.

There were times—perhaps there still are—when we were not always certain which force was which, but we learned from this tragedy some truths about ourselves that had never before been disclosed to us, or that we had never before been willing to confront.

We learned that we had the strength and goodness, as a nation, to create a political leader the world could not only respect but admire. And we learned that we had within us the sickness and depravity that could spawn the destruction of our own best creations. We wept not only for the loss of John Kennedy, but for the loss of our national innocence and naivete as well.

And as the nation wept, it turned to the heroine of the tragedy, Jacqueline Kennedy, for consolation and re-assurance, and found it.

Every eye in America was fixed upon this young and beautiful widow during the dark days that followed the assassination. We watched in wonder and admiration as she bore herself through the ordeal of her husband's death and his elaborate funeral with a grace and poise we had no right to demand of anyone, but that we were grateful to discover in her.

So expertly did Jackie Kennedy play her part in the drama that we almost forgot at times that there was more to her than a public face and a public posture, that beneath lay a real woman vulnerable to the passions, fears, torments and anguish of real people.

Most of us did not want that reality to break through during the days following the assassination. We were watching a tragedy, and we demanded that all its partici-pants play their roles well. To a remarkable degree, Mrs. Kennedy seemed to sense her responsibility to re-main in character at all times. Her every movement, her every gesture, her every public word seemed tuned to the role fate had cast upon her.

But the curtain now has fallen. The drama has ended and the audience has filed out of the theater and gone back to its more mundane pursuits. We can now look backstage for the real woman who played so magnifi-cently during those four or five days of tragedy.

She is there, if one looks closely enough, make no mis-take about it. This was not a woman who was poised and graceful because she was unmoved. This was a woman who had summoned, in spite of her human vulnerability to tragedy, the strength she and we needed at that mo-ment.

Jackie Kennedy was no stranger to tragedy and its

demands. On Aug. 9, 1963, her two-day-old son, Patrick, died of a relatively rare respiratory disease of infancy. Another child, a girl, had been stillborn in 1956.

But for a time, her life had been one of ease and plenty. Born in 1929 in the luxury of East Hampton, Long Island, she attended good private schools, and completed her formal education at Vassar, the Sorbonne in Paris and George Washington University.

While working as an inquiring photographer for the now defunct Washington Times-Herald, Jackie met John F. Kennedy, then a young congressman from Massachusetts. They were married on Sept. 12, 1953, in plush Newport, Rhode Island.

When John Kennedy was elected President, it seemed as if Jackie had been born to become the First Lady. She brought a lively new spirit of culture and elegance to the White House and quickly won the admiration and affection not only of the American people, but of people all over the world.

Jackie accompanied the President on few of his official trips. She was not, as Kenneth P. O'Donnell, a close friend and adviser of Mr. Kennedy's, said, "a girl who had loved campaigning." But when she did travel with her husband, she drew tremendously enthusiastic crowds. On President Kennedy's trip to Paris and Vienna in 1961, Jackie, who is fluent in French and Spanish, all but outshone the President in the eyes of the adoring Frenchmen.

In November, 1963, when President Kennedy embarked on his swing through Texas, Jackie was at his side.

Her own description of what happened on November 22 took but 10 minutes to tell to the Warren Commission. Her words, like the woman herself, are poignant, gentle and imbued with a natural dignity that clashes at times with the formal manner of her questioners.

Jackie's testimony to the Warren Commission was given at her home in Georgetown. J. Lee Rankin, the Commission's chief counsel, did the questioning. Earl Warren, the Commission chairman, and Robert F. Kennedy, upon whom Jackie had leaned so heavily since the assassination of her husband, also were present. The small group sat in the living room of the old Georgetown house, filled with its many mementos of the dead President, as Jackie spoke softly about the day her husband died.

The session was begun by Earl Warren.

"Mrs. Kennedy," he said, "the Commission would like to have you say in your own words, in your own way, what happened at the time of the assassination of the President. Mr. Rankin will ask you a few questions, just from the time you left the airport until the time you started for the hospital. And we want it to be brief. We want it to be in your own words and want you to say anything that you feel is appropriate to that occasion."

With that introduction, Warren inducted Mrs. Kennedy as a witness before the Commission and Rankin took her through the formalities of stating her name and declaring that she was "the widow of the former President Kennedy."

"Can you go back to the time that you came to Love Field on Nov. 22," Rankin asked, "and describe what happened there after you landed in the plane?"

"We got off the plane," Mrs. Kennedy said. "The then Vice President and Mrs. Johnson were there. They gave us flowers. And then the car was waiting, but there was a big crowd there, all yelling, with banners and everything. And we went to shake hands with them. It was a very hot day. And you went along a long line. I tried to stay close to my husband and lots of times you get pushed away, you know, people leaning over and pulling your hand. They were very friendly.

"And, finally, I don't know how we got back to the car. I think Congressman Thomas somehow was helping me. There was lots of confusion."

Rankin confirmed with Mrs. Kennedy the seating arrangement in the Presidential car, and Jackie described the motorcade into Dallas.

"As you got into the main street of Dallas, were there very large crowds on all the streets?" Rankin asked.

"Yes," Jackie replied.

"And you waved to them and proceeded down the street with the motorcade?"

"Yes. And in the motorcade, you know, I usually would be waving mostly to the left side and he was waving mostly to the right, which is one reason you are not looking at each other very much. And it was terribly hot. Just blinding all of us."

As we shall see in a moment, Jackie is haunted by the idea that if she had been looking to her right, she might have helped save her husband's life.

"Now do you remember as you turned off of the main street into Houston Street?" Rankin asked.

"I don't know the name of the street," Jackie apologized.

Rankin explained that Houston was the street they were on just before they turned to pass the book depository, and Jackie responded: "Well, I remember whenever it was, Mrs. Connally said, 'We will soon be there.' We could see a tunnel in front of us. Everything was really slow then. And I remember thinking it would be so cool under that tunnel."

With Rankin leading her, Mrs. Kennedy recalled Mrs. Connally's comment to President Kennedy about the warm welcome Dallas was giving him, and suddenly she is at the moment of the assassination.

"And then," she says, "do you want me to tell you what happened?"

"Yes," Rankin says, "if you would, please."

"You know, there is always noise in a motorcade and there are always motorcycles beside us, a lot of them backfiring. So I was looking to the left, I guess there was a noise, but it didn't seem like any different noise really because there is so much noise, motorcycles and things. But then suddenly Governor Connally was yelling, 'Oh, no, no, no.'"

Rankin breaks in. "Did he turn toward you?" he asks.

"No," Jackie says. "I was looking this way, to the left, and I heard these terrible noises. You know. And my husband never made any sound. So I turned to the right. And all I remember is seeing my husband, he had this sort of quizzical look on his face, and his hand was up, it must have been his left hand. And just as I turned and looked at him, I could see a piece of his skull and I remember it was flesh colored. I remember thinking he just looked as if he had a slight headache. I just remember seeing that. No blood or anything.

"And then he sort of did this, put his hand to his forehead and fell in my lap.

"And then I just remember falling on him and saying, 'Oh, no, no, no,' I mean 'Oh, my God, they have shot my husband,' and 'I love you, Jack.' I remember I was shouting. And just being down in the car with his head in my lap. And it just seemed an eternity.

"You know, then, there were pictures later on of me climbing out the back. But I don't remember that at all."

"Do you remember Mr. Hill coming to try to help on the car?" Rankin asked.

"I don't remember anything," Jackie said. "I was just down like that, and then I remember a voice behind me, or something, and then I remember the people in the front seat, or somebody, finally knew something was wrong, and a voice yelling, which must have been Mr. Hill, 'get to the hospital,' or maybe it was Mr. Kellerman, in the front seat. But someone yelling. I was just down and holding him."

At this point, as we have seen, Mrs. Kennedy's description of her husband's wounds was deleted from the published record.

Rankin then asked Mrs. Kennedy how many shots she heard.

"Well," she replied, "there must have been two because the one that made me turn around was Governor Connally yelling. And it used to confuse me because first I remembered there were three and I used to think my husband didn't make any sound when he was shot. And Governor Connally screamed. And then I read the other day that it was the same shot that hit them both.

"But I used to think if I only had been looking to the right, I would have seen the first shot hit him, then I could have pulled him down, and then the second shot would not have hit him. But I heard Governor Connally yelling and that made me turn around, and as I turned to the right, my husband was doing this," she said, holding her hand to her neck. "He was receiving a bullet. And those are the only two I remember.

"And I read there was a third shot. But I don't know.

"Just those two."

It is a calm, almost detached description that Jackie gives of her husband's murder. The performance continues for her up to this moment.

But from others we get a more intimate look.

Lady Bird Johnson dictated her recollections of that "fateful and dreadful day," as she called it, into a tape recorder eight days after the assassination.

"I did this primarily as a form of therapy—to help me get over the shock and horror of the experience of President Kennedy's assassination," she told Earl Warren in submitting a transcript of the tape recording to the Commission.

Mrs. Johnson said in her statement that her first glimpse of Jackie on the afternoon of Nov. 22, 1963, came as the car in which she and her husband had been riding arrived at Parkland Hospital.

"As we ground to a halt," Lady Bird said, "Secret Service men began to pull, lead, guide and hustle us out. I cast one last look over my shoulder and saw, in the President's car, a bundle of pink, just like a drift of blossoms, lying on the back seat. I think it was Mrs. Kennedy lying over the President's body."

Later, Mrs. Johnson said, she asked to see Mrs. Kennedy in the hospital. Secret Service men "began to lead me up one corridor .... and down another. Suddenly I found myself face to face with Jackie in a small hall. I think it was right outside the operating room."

"You always think of her—or someone like her—as being insulated, protected," Mrs. Johnson said. "She was quite alone. I don't think I ever saw anyone so much alone in my life. I went up to her, put my arms around her, and said something to her. I'm sure it was something like, 'God help us all,' because my feelings for her were too tumultuous to put into words."

The new First Lady and the former First Lady met again aboard Air Force One, the Presidential plane, shortly after Kennedy's body had been placed on the aircraft and Lyndon Johnson had been sworn into office as President.

"We all sat around the plane," Mrs. Johnson said. "We had at first been ushered into the main private Presidential cabin on the plane—but Lyndon quickly said, 'no, no,' and immediately led us out of there; we felt that is where Mrs. Kennedy should be. The casket was in the hall. I went in to see Mrs. Kennedy, and though it was a very hard thing to do, she made it as easy as possible.

"She said things like, 'Oh, Lady Bird, it's good that we've always liked you two so much.' She said, 'Oh, what if I had not been there? I'm so glad I was there.'

"I looked at her. Mrs. Kennedy's dress was stained with blood. Her right glove was caked—that immaculate woman—it was caked with blood, her husband's blood. She always wore gloves like she was used to them. I never could.

"Somehow that was one of the most poignant sights—exquisitely dressed and caked in blood.

"I asked her if I couldn't get someone in to help her change, and she said, 'Oh, no. Perhaps later I'll ask Mary Gallagher, but not right now.'"

Jackie never changed her clothes that night. She continued to wear the blood-stained pink suit as a talisman of terror until she returned to the White House at about 5 o'clock the next morning.

Mrs. Johnson removed a paragraph from her statement

that explained why Jackie refused to change her clothes. "And then," the deleted paragraph said, "with something —if you can say a person that gentle, that dignified, you can say had an element of fierceness—she said, 'I want them to see what they have done to Jack.'"

Jackie made another fierce and pitiful outcry heard by Governor Connally and his wife during the actual shooting. After the shot that blew Kennedy's skull apart, Jackie screamed: "They have killed my husband. I have his brains in my hand."

Jackie doesn't remember much of what happened during the assassination. She is totally unable to recall climbing to the trunk of the Presidential limousine and being saved from falling by Secret Service man Clinton Hill. But Hill gave what may be a clue to her strange behavior.

Hill said that after he heard the first shot, he ran to the President's car, which was then only about five feet in front of the Secret Service followup car.

"Just about as I reached it," Hill said, "there was another sound, which was different than the first sound. I think I described it in my statement as though someone was shooting a revolver into a hard object—it seemed to have some type of an echo.

"I put my right foot, I believe it was, on the left rear step of the automobile, and I had a hold of the handgrip with my hand, when the car lurched forward. I lost my footing and I had to run about three or four more steps before I could get back up on the car.

"Between the time I originally grabbed the handhold and until I was up on the car, Mrs. Kennedy—the second noise that I heard had removed a portion of the President's head, and he had slumped noticeably to his left, Mrs. Kennedy had jumped up from the seat and was, it appeared to me, reaching for something coming off the right rear bumper of the car, the right rear tail, when she noticed that I was trying to climb on the car.

"She turned toward me and I grabbed her and put her

back in the back seat, crawled up on top of the back seat and lay there."

Arlen Specter, a Commission assistant counsel, asked Hill whether he knew what Mrs. Kennedy might have been reaching for.

"I thought I saw something come off the back, too," Hill said, "but I cannot say that there was. I do know that the next day, we found a portion of the President's head .... It was found in the street. It was turned in, I believe, by a medical student or somebody in Dallas...."

Returning to his rescue of Mrs. Kennedy, Hill said he "simply just pushed" her back into the seat "and she moved—somewhat voluntarily—right back into the same seat she was in. The President—when she had attempted to get out onto the trunk of the car, his body apparently did not move too much, because when she got back into the car, he was at that time, when I got on top of the car, face up in her lap."

Hill said that when he reached the rear of the President's car, he heard Jackie crying, "My God, they have shot his head off," and on the way to the hospital, he heard her say, "Jack, Jack, what have they done to you?" and he heard her sob.

At Parkland, Hill said, Jackie immediately went into the emergency room with her husband and remained there "until she was convinced to wait outside, which she did, remained there the rest of the period of time that we were there."

Roy Kellerman, the Secret Service man in the front seat of the President's car and the only witness who heard Kennedy say, "My God, I am hit," after the first shot, also heard Jackie say, "What are they doing to you?" as the bullets flew into the car.

Kenneth O'Donnell spent more time with Jackie than anyone else during the agonizing hours that followed the assassination.

O'Donnell had been riding in the followup car with Hill and the other Secret Service agents, and had witnessed the scene in which Jackie climbed to the trunk of Kennedy's car.

Later, at Parkland, he said, he "went right to Mrs. Kennedy. She was seated right outside the room where they had placed the President. I would say she was in a total daze, and as yet not knowing whether there was any hope or not."

O'Donnell stayed with Jackie for a few minutes, then went into the emergency room and discussed President Kennedy's condition with the doctors. "I said, 'I think we better get a definite answer one way or another —is there any hope at all?' I was unable to get a conclusive answer. But I think I got the answer I needed.

"I don't know how Mrs. Kennedy was finally told. I may have told her about at that moment."

After hurrying to see Johnson and making plans for the new President's departure from Dallas, O'Donnell returned to Mrs. Kennedy, "who was in a very understandably distraught condition."

"It was my opinion—I tried to in some way imply that she might leave and come with us, at least to get her out of that room. She was covered with blood. . . . Her response to me was she would not leave her huband's body. At that point, I realized that she would not. The doctors had continually attempted to get her to take some form of sedation. And she had consistently refused, and told me she would not take anything, that she was going to stay with her husband.

"I realized that she was going to stay with her husband, no matter what anybody did, and there was no possible way of in any way getting her to leave. And so, therefore, the only alternative I could see was that we move the President."

O'Donnell left Mrs. Kennedy sitting in the corridor of the emergency room and went to arrange for a casket to be brought to the hospital.

"It seems to me it wasn't more than half an hour that they arrived with the casket," O'Donnell recalled. "I remember just before they arrived I got Dave Powers (another close friend of the President) and said there was a little room in the back that we ought to just take Mrs. Kennedy under some subterfuge, and talk to her in the room while we brought the casket in, because I thought that might be the final blow. And we did, and—but she knew what was going on. She came out and said, 'No, I want to watch it all.' And she stood in the doorway, and thanked us for our attempt at being compassionate."

At about this time, Mrs. Kennedy quietly entered the emergency room and, in a simple gesture that literally made a nation gasp with sympathy, placed her wedding ring in the hand of her dead husband.

As if Mrs. Kennedy's grief were not unbearable enough already, she was now forced to witness another of those ghastly ineptitudes so frequently displayed by Dallas authorities that day.

As the President's body was being wheeled out of the emergency room, "a gentleman arrived who said that we would not be allowed to remove the body from the hospital until the necessary papers had been signed," O'Donnell said.

O'Donnell didn't know who the man was, but assumed he was a representative of the coroner's office.

"We asked—I don't recollect who transmitted the message—that they speed this up as much as possible, and give us some idea how long it took to accomplish this. And they went out into this other little room where there were some telephones and proceeded to call whoever it was necessary to call in order to get this permission."

O'Donnell said he waited 10 to 15 minutes, then asked the local official if he had an answer. "Nobody seemed to be able to answer the question as to how long it might take, and whether it was a week or an hour," O'Donnell said.

"So I was getting more concerned about Mrs. Kennedy's state all the time—although she appeared composed, as she had from the beginning."

Finally, a man O'Donnell identified as a Judge Brown arrived and told him that "as of now this was just a homicide case and there were certain things that had to be carried out, one of which I interpreted as an autopsy. . . . I realized we were talking not about hours, but perhaps even days, which was an impossible situation for Mrs. Kennedy."

O'Donnell offered to take a Dallas doctor along to Washington to aid in the performance of the autopsy there, but this offer was refused.

"I in my own mind determined that we had no alternative but to just depart," O'Donnell said. "So I went back in the room. I told Mr. O'Brien (another Presidential assistant) and whoever else was assembled there that we were going to leave. I notified the Secret Service . . . . and told them to get ready to depart. We went in and took the body out. Mrs. Kennedy stood right behind it, I think totally unaware of the problems that were then existing, so perhaps confused as to the speed with which we were attempting to depart.

"We pushed the casket out through the hall. This first gentleman that had come in, who, I presume, was from the coroner's office, shouted very loudly, 'You can't do that, you can't leave here now.' Nobody paid any attention to him. We pushed through another set of swinging doors. I remember a Catholic priest was between this and the doorway, and was praying. It was most disconcerting because we were concerned at all times that some moment they would say stop, and I hated to think what might happen to Mrs. Kennedy if she had to go back and go through all this over again. So we brushed them all aside and came out the same way we had come in, through the same doors."

Secret Service agent Kellerman was involved in this grotesque episode.

He said he was approached at the hospital by a man who represented himself as an official of the local Health Department.

Kellerman said the official told him: "There has been

a homicide here. You won't be able to remove the body. We will have to take it down there to the mortuary and have an autopsy."

"I said, 'No, we are not,'" Kellerman recalled. "And he said, 'We have a law here, whereby you have to comply with it.'"

At this point, Kellerman said, a physician walked into the room, "and I said, 'Doctor, this man is from some health unit in town. He tells me we can't remove this body.' The doctor became a little enraged; he said, 'We are removing it.' He said, 'This is the President of the United States and there should be some consideration in an event like this.'

"And I told this gentleman, I said, 'You are going to have to come up with something a little stronger than you to give us the law that this body can't be removed.'"

Kellerman said the local health officer "frantically called everybody he could think of," but was unable to reach any important public official. Eventually, however, the man found Judge Brown, who supported the health official's demand that the body remain in Dallas for an autopsy. But Kellerman stood firm. "It doesn't make any difference," he said. "We are going to move it."

With that, the casket bearing Kennedy's body was rolled down the hall and Kellerman got into the ambulance with Mrs. Kennedy and other members of the Presidential party.

Even then, the local officials would not abandon their petty point. As the ambulance was pulling away from the hospital, Kellerman said, "a gentleman taps on the driver's window and they roll it down and he says, 'I will meet you at the mortuary.'"

"Yes, sir," Kellerman muttered. But he had no intention of complying with these absurd instructions. "We went to the airport, gentlemen," he told the Warren Commission.

In the Presidential plane during that gloomy flight back to Washington, O'Donnell sat with Jackie in a secluded cabin and talked.

"The President called me up on one or two occasions and asked me to stay up in the cabin, wanted to talk to me, but I felt I had to stay with Mrs. Kennedy. So I sat with her the whole trip," O'Donnell said.

"What did you talk about?" Arlen Specter asked.

"We reminisced," O'Donnell said.

"Did she have anything to eat on the trip back?" Specter asked. The question seems a trifle irrelevant to a discussion of the assassination, but O'Donnell answered it.

"No," he said. "I think we both had a drink. I tried to get her to take a good strong drink. I had not much luck."

Not satisfied with O'Donnell's reply, Specter persisted.

"She drank part but not all?" he asked.

"As I recollect," O'Donnell said parrying the question adroitly, "she just wanted to talk. She talked all the way."

Once back in Washington, the grieving widow again walked onto the stage of history.

Who can forget the television pictures of her disembarking from the Presidential plane behind her husband's coffin, still wearing her blood-smeared pink suit, fumbling for a moment to find the door of the ambulance, and driving into the darkness while the camera's eye turned toward Lyndon Johnson issuing his first public pronouncement as President? Who can forget the heavily veiled woman walking with a certain pride at the head of a procession of world leaders to her husband's funeral, or standing on the steps of the Capitol flanked by her young son and daughter, or kneeling beside the President's flag-draped coffin in the Rotunda and kissing it?

Those who lived through that awful week in November, 1963, will carry such images in their minds to their dying day. They are images we cannot erase because, in their way, they are glimpses of a kind of greatness.

Chapter Eight

Marina: The Mystery Witness

For a moment on the night of November 21, 1963, John Kennedy's life and the course of the nation's history hung on a wife's reply to her husband's pleas for reconciliation.

The wife, Marina Oswald, answered waspishly and her husband murdered the President. Had her response been different at that critical moment, Lee Oswald might well have abandoned his plan to assassinate Kennedy.

The crucial conversation took place in Mrs. Ruth Paine's house in Irving, Texas, the Dallas suburb where Marina and her baby had been living for the previous two months.

It was a Thursday night. Oswald normally visited Marina only on weekends. But this was no ordinary Thursday night. Kennedy was coming to Dallas the next day, and Oswald's rifle was hidden in Mrs. Paine's garage.

Accompanying Oswald's plans for assassinating the President were the clangorous sounds of discord that filled his relationship with Marina.

There had been a nasty blowup earlier that week when Marina had discovered that Oswald was living in Dallas under an assumed name. Using a phone number Oswald had given her, Mrs. Paine had called him at Marina's request. Mrs. Paine was informed that no one by the name of Lee Oswald lived at that address. When Oswald called Marina the following day, she demanded an explanation.

Oswald told his wife he had registered in the rooming house on North Beckley Avenue under the name of O.H. Lee (Lee Harvey Oswald backwards) because he did not want people to find out he had lived in Russia. He asked Marina to erase his phone number from Mrs. Paine's address book, Marina refused and an argument erupted. "He insisted," Marina said, "and I said that he was stupid and hung up."

Three days later, on Nov. 21, Oswald showed up at Mrs. Paine's house. When Marina asked him why he had come during the week, he said "he was lonely" and "wanted to make his peace with me," Marina recalled.

"He tried to talk to me but I would not answer him, and he was very upset," Marina told the Warren Commission. "I was angry, of course. He was not angry. He was upset. I was angry. . . ."

"How did you indicate to him that you were angry?" she was asked.

"By not talking to him," she said.

Despite Marina's obstinate silence, Oswald urged her to end their separation and move into an apartment in Dallas with him. "He said he was tired of living alone and perhaps the reason for my being so angry was the fact that we were not living together; that if I want to, he would rent an apartment in Dallas tomorrow; that he didn't want me to remain with Ruth any longer, but wanted me to live with him in Dallas.

"He repeated this not once but several times, but I refused. And he said that once again I was preferring my friends to him, and that I didn't need him."

Marina was unmoved.

"I said it would be better if I remained with Ruth until the holidays. He would come, we would all meet together; that this was better because while he was living alone and I stayed with Ruth, we were spending less money. And I told him to buy me a washing machine, because with two children it became too difficult to wash by hand."

"What did he say to that?" asked the Commission's chief counsel, J. Lee Rankin.

"He said he would buy me a washing machine," Marina replied.

"What did you say to that?"

"Thank you," Marina said. "That it would be better if he bought something for himself—that I would manage."

With this snappish remark, the conversation ended abruptly. Oswald "stopped talking and sat down and watched television and then went to bed," Marina said. "I went to bed later. It was about 9 o'clock when he went to sleep. I went to sleep about 11:30. But it seemed to me that he was not really asleep. But I didn't talk to him.

"In the morning, he got up, said goodbye, and left, and that I shouldn't get up—as always, I did not get up to prepare breakfast. This was quite usual."

Looking at this conversation in the context of what happened the next day, it seems as if Oswald were seeking a way out of his commitment to murder the President by trying to project his life beyond November 22. His wife would have no part of it, however. His attempt to find some reason to avoid bringing his life down in rubble failed. The plans he had made—or that had been made for him—would not be altered.

If Marina had agreed that night to a reconciliation, the assassination might never have taken place.

Marina herself sensed in retrospect the critical nature of that conversation with her husband on the eve of the President's murder.

"Of course," she told the Warren Commission, "if I had known what was going to happen, I would have agreed without further thought. Perhaps, if Lee was planning anything, he staked everything on a card. That is, if I agreed to his proposal to go with him to Dallas, he would not do what he had planned, and if I did not, then he would."

Probably no single witness did more to convince the Warren Commission of Lee Oswald's guilt than his wife.

She told the Commission that Oswald had attempted to murder General Walker, thus providing proof of her husband's "capacity for violence," and casting him in the role of a potential assassin. She authenticated two highly incriminating photographs, showing Oswald holding the rifle used in the assassination, by describing in detail how she had taken the pictures. She identified the rifle found in the book depository as belonging to Oswald.

Repeatedly, she provided damning little insights to Oswald's life and personality that helped the Commission weld the tangible evidence against him into the final portrait of a killer.

Marina's behavior before the Warren Commission is enigmatic. Oswald's mother took the more predictable course. Although eccentric and at times hysterical, she insisted on her son's innocence, hired lawyers to defend his name, fought like a wounded animal protecting its young—all to prove he was a victim rather than an assassin.

One might have expected Marina to follow a similar path, or at least to remain neutral—to offer a minimum of aid to investigators, to answer questions innocuously, to volunteer almost nothing incriminating, and even to color her statements about her husband with favorable hues.

Marina employed none of these evasive or deceptive tactics. Instead, she told the Commission everything any prosecutor could hope to hear, bathed Oswald in the most damaging light, and finally asserted that she was convinced of her husband's guilt.

Marina's cooperative attitude toward the Warren Commission is even more remarkable when it is recalled that she was the product of a hostile social system and might understandably have reflected some of that hostility toward a United States government panel which sought to prove her husband guilty of the most heinous crime of the century.

If Oswald had lived to stand trial, it is unlikely that a jury would have heard a word of Marina's testimony. In American law, a wife cannot be compelled to testify against her husband, and Marina certainly would have been kept from the witness stand by Oswald's lawyers. If she had insisted for some reason on testifying for the prosecution, she would have been subjected to as merciless a cross-examination as any American courtroom had ever witnessed.

Because of her Russian background, Marina assumed for some a slightly sinister role in the assassination drama. Almost from the start, there were simmering suspicions that she was a Soviet agent, that she was a CIA agent, that she had been recruited by the FBI. These suspicions probably are nonsense, but there are two aspects of her life after the assassination that are curious and worth noting.

First, she was kept under very close watch by the Secret Service after President Kennedy's murder, questioned for many hours at a time, and certainly coached on her testimony.

During this time, no doubt, she was subjected to subtle and overt pressures to cooperate. As we shall see later, she complained about such pressure exerted by the FBI, but she had only praise for the Secret Service, which presumably handles these matters with more delicacy.

Second, there is a strange if remote link between Marina and Jack Ruby, Oswald's killer. When Ruby's roommate, George Senator, heard that Ruby had shot Oswald on November 24, he immediately sought advice from James Martin, a Dallas lawyer and acquaintance of Ruby. Although Martin declined to represent Ruby, he turns up in the case a few months later—as the man selected by the Secret Service to act as Marina Oswald's business manager and personal adviser. Here too we get a hint of an explanation for Marina's unexpected cooperation with the investigators. Undoubtedly, Martin advised Marina repeatedly that it was in her best interest to cooperate fully with the authorities.

Who is Marina Oswald? Perhaps by finding out a little about her background and by looking at what she said about herself and what others said about her, we can understand her and her actions better.

The circumstances of Marina Nikolayevna Prusakova's birth are left somewhat uncertain by the Warren Commission.

"She was born," the Commission says, "on July 17, 1941, at Sverodyinsk, Arkhangel Oblast, Russia. A few years later, her mother, Klavdiya Vasilievna Prusakova, married Aleksandr Ivanovich Medvedev, who became the only father Marina knew."

Marina was raised by her maternal grandparents until she was about seven, then by her mother and stepfather, who Marina told the Commission were not members of the Communist Party.

For a time, the family lived in the Moldavian region of the Soviet Union, then moved to Leningrad, Russia's second city, where Marina completed the seventh grade and was trained as a pharmacist.

Upon graduating from the Pharmacy Teknikum in 1959, Marina got a job in a pharmaceutical warehouse in Leningrad. She worked there just one day, then quit. After two months of idleness, punctuated by disagreements with her stepfather, she went to Minsk to live with an aunt and uncle.

Her uncle was a Communist Party member employed by the MVD or Ministry of Internal Affairs.

Marina went to work in the drug department of a Minsk hospital, joined the local Komsomol—the Communist youth organization—and fell in with a group of young adults who, as she put it, "ran together."

Seven months after her arrival in Minsk, Marina met Lee Oswald at a dance. At first she thought he came from one of the Baltic states because he spoke Russian with an accent. But later that evening, Oswald told her he was an American.

Oswald, on the rebound from an unsuccessful romance

with another girl he had hoped to marry, arranged to meet Marina at a dance the following week. At this second meeting, they agreed to see each other again a week later. But before the week was out, Oswald had fallen ill with a polyp condition and had entered a Minsk hospital.

During the next few days, Marina visited Oswald often at the hospital, using her medical uniform to get into his room even when visitors were not allowed. By the time Oswald was discharged from the hospital, he had asked Marina to marry him.

Marina was cool to the idea at first, but as they spent more time together, Oswald's ardor warmed her. They were married in Minsk on April 30, 1961, and after a three-day honeymoon which they spent in the Byelorussian capital, they settled down to the life of a young married couple in the Soviet Union.

Unknown to Marina, however, Oswald had long since grown tired of Soviet society and within only a month or two after the marriage, he told Marina he wanted to return to the United States.

Marina did not oppose the plan, and for the next year, Oswald and his wife wrestled with the mass of red-tape blocking their departure from the Soviet Union and their entry into the United States. During this year Marina became pregnant and gave birth to a baby girl in February. Finally, on June 2, 1962, Oswald, his wife and their young daughter crossed the Soviet border at Brest, took a train to Amsterdam, boarded the Dutch liner Maasdam, and sailed for New York.

From there, Oswald and his family went to Fort Worth, where they lived for a time with Oswald's brother, Robert.

During the next few months, Oswald and Marina moved repeatedly, first to an apartment with his mother, then into a small apartment of their own, to Dallas, to New Orleans, and finally back to Dallas.

Soon after they arrived in Texas, their marriage began

running seriously afoul. Oswald objected to Marina's friends, mainly members of the Russian-speaking community in Dallas-Fort Worth. He got angry when she smoked, and he once hit her when he discovered she had written a letter to an old boyfriend in Russia saying she was sorry she hadn't married him instead of Lee Oswald. Marina's account of this incident is interesting. She says she deserved to be beaten for what she had done.

"Once we had a quarrel because I had a young man who was a boyfriend—this was before we were married, a boy who was in love with me, and I liked him, too," she told the Warren Commission. "And I had written him a letter from here. I had—I wrote him that I was very lonely here, that Lee had changed a great deal, and that I was sorry that I had not married him instead, that it would have been so much easier for me.

"I had mailed that letter showing the post-office box as a return address. But this was just the time when the postage rates went up by one cent, and the letter was returned. Lee brought that letter and asked me what it was and forced me to read it. But I refused.

"Then he sat down across from me and started to read it to me. I was very much ashamed of my foolishness. And, of course, he hit me, but he did not believe that this letter was sincere. He asked me if it was true or not, and I told him it was true. But he thought that I did it only in order to tease him. And that was the end of it. It was a very ill-considered thing."

Asked if she recalled any more about this incident, Marina added:

"Of course after he hit me, he said that I should be ashamed of myself for saying such things because he was very much in love with me. But this was after he hit me.

"Generally I think that was right, for such things, that is the right thing to do. There was some grounds for it."

In the months that followed, Oswald seemed to grow tenser and more irritable, and finally, Marina left him. But she stayed away only a week and returned. The bickering continued, however, and at the time of the assassination, Oswald was living in a room in Dallas and Marina and their two daughters were staying with Mrs. Ruth Paine in Irving.

Marina everywhere depicted herself as an undemanding wife and she denied she badgered Oswald to earn more money and provide her with more comforts. Her friends offer a different view.

George De Mohrenschildt, a member of the Russian emigré community who befriended the Oswalds, told the Warren Commission Marina kept up a constant barrage about Oswald's inability to earn more money.

"'—Why don't you make some money?' Why don't they have a car, why don't they have more dresses, look at everybody else living so well, and they are just miserable flunkies" was the refrain De Mohrenschildt said he heard from Marina. "She was annoying him all the time," De Mohrenschildt said. "Poor guy was going out of his mind."

De Mohrenschildt's wife, Jeanne, corroborated her husband's account. "I have the impression that he was just pushed, pushed, pushed, pushed," she said of Oswald, "and she was probably nagging, nagging, nagging, nagging."

De Mohrenschildt said he and his wife urged Marina to relax her pressure on Oswald but their efforts were futile.

He also recalled another "annoying thing" about Marina's behavior toward her husband.

"She openly said he didn't see her physically," De Mohrenschildt said, "right in front of him. She said, 'He sleeps with me just once a month, and I never get any satisfaction out of it.' A rather crude and completely straightforward thing to say in front of relative strangers, as we were."

Elena Hall, another Russian emigré, also heard Marina complain about her sex life with Oswald.

"Did she ever tell you that Oswald would—was not very much of a man in that sense?" a Commission lawyer asked her.

"Yes, that is what she told me," Mrs. Hall said.

"They very seldom had sexual relations?" the lawyer asked.

"Yes, sir," Mrs. Hall replied.

Mrs. Hall, De Mohrenschildt, his wife and others reported to the Commission that Marina frequently made fun of Oswald in front of outsiders, ridiculed him and, as Mrs. Hall put it, "she would pick up something little and go on and have an argument for nothing. . . ."

Perhaps the best insight to Marina's personality, or at least to her own view of herself, can be found in an autobiographical sketch she prepared for the Warren Commission.

The sketch shows hints, from its style and organization, that Marina had help in preparing it, probably from the Secret Service or her business manager, James Martin.

Fate, Marina says in this autobiography, brought her and Lee Oswald together in Minsk in the winter of 1961. Among all the people in this city of 500,000, she observes wistfully, "two found each other: Myself, a Russian—my future husband, an American. We represented different worlds, different continents, but we were united by fate."

Marina, who describes herself at the time as "a frivolous girl," tells of her meeting with Oswald at the dance in the Minsk Palace of Culture. "I liked Lee immediately," she writes. "He was very polite and attentive, and I felt that he liked me too, since he tried not to miss any dances with me. He got nervous if anyone else managed to invite me first.

"Later, when we were married, Lee told me that he noticed me as soon as I came into the dance hall. Don't think that I have an especially high opinion of myself or am anything unusual, but I can say that my youth, and the fact that I had just come in from the cold—had their effect.

"By then the girls were already tired, whereas I had just taken off my overcoat—so that I had a fresh look and was not pale like the others. I remember having on my favorite dress made of red Chinese brocade—Lee liked this dress afterwards—and my hair was done a la Brigitte Bardot. That evening I even liked myself. You see how I am boasting; but I am writing what I felt."

When Marina brought Oswald home with her after the dance the following week, she writes that her aunt liked "his modesty and politeness, also the fact that he was very neat. She told me with a laugh that only an American was lacking in my collection."

At first, Marina writes, she was sorry for Oswald, rather than in love with him, because he was "completely alone although he had friends." But later her sympathy turned to love, and she describes how they spent long evenings together in Oswald's Minsk apartment.

"I remember one of those evenings when we drank tea with pastry and kisses," she says. "Ten—please excuse my vulgarity due to youth—the tea was very tasty. I never again drank such tea or ate such pastry—ha, ha."

The bliss was shortlived, however. Oswald enjoyed classical music. Marina writes, and became enamored of an opera called "The Queen of Spades." They argued over his fondness for this opera, which Marina said he would play on a phonograph four or five times in an evening. Marina's aunt noticed the newly discordant tone of their relationship, and warned Marina not to bother Oswald "with little things."

Marina also grew disturbed about Oswald's reaction to the birth of their first child. Oswald showered his daughter, June, with affection from the moment of her birth, but Marina was concerned because it seemed to her "that he didn't love me any more, but just the daughter."

The trouble got worse after Marina and Oswald settled in Texas. Oswald disagreed with Marina's friends about political issues, Marina writes, and because of this "he started being disagreeable to my friends and even to me, because I tried to maintain contact with them. I was hurt that Lee so avoided people and wanted me to do the same. We started to quarrel.

"In general our family life began to deteriorate after we arrived in America. Lee was always hot-tempered, and now this trait of character more and more prevented us from living together in harmony."

Unlike her friends, who place much of the blame for her marital difficulties on her shoulders, she absolves herself completely.

"We quarreled only because he had a difficult character and because that was the only way he could love," she says. "But he did not think that these quarrels could break up the family, and so I forgave him everything."

As Marina's narrative of her life moves closer to the day of the assassination, she becomes progressively more hostile toward her husband.

Describing a fight she had with Oswald because he had told a landlady his wife was Czechoslovakian, Marina writes that she left Oswald after denouncing him as "simply stupid." When Oswald asked her to return to him, she refused "since I wanted to show him that I had a character too as well as self-respect, and that he couldn't trample on this self-respect too much."

"Of course my heart wanted to return to him" she writes, "but I didn't try to show him this. I wanted him to see that family life is not a plaything, and that he had to be more serious about it.

"Then it seemed to me that Lee didn't love me any more and although it was very hard to turn him down, I told him that I didn't want to live any longer with a person who hurt me without any reason, and that I wanted a divorce.

"I saw that Lee went home extremely upset, and I felt that this might teach him a lesson. Of course, I did not want a divorce, since I loved Lee, but I would have done it if he had not so insisted and begged me to come home."

They did not get a divorce. Marina relented and returned to live with Oswald because "I felt that this man is very unhappy, and that he cannot love in any other way .... I saw that if I did not go back to him, things would be very hard for him .... I felt for the first time that this person was not born to live among people, that among them he was alone. I was sorry for him and frightened. I was afraid that if I did not go back to him something might happen. I didn't have anything concrete in mind, but my intuition told me that I couldn't do this. Not because I am anything special, but I knew that he needed me. I went back to Lee."

Marina says, again in sharp contradiction of her friends, that she was not concerned about luxuries, but that Oswald was "terribly unhappy that he could not give those things which other husbands can give their wives."

"Lee suspected—although there was no reason for it—that I blamed him for his inability to get along in life. And because he thought about this more than I did, he used to get angry at me and would criticize me for my friends. Again we quarreled, but I forget hurts quickly and was ready to forgive—especially my unsuccessful husband."

Marina recalls her enjoyment of the 1962 Thanksgiving holiday, which she and Oswald spent with Lee's brother, and of the fun they had at Christmas, which they celebrated with friends. But New Year's Eve "was very dull for us as we stayed home," she writes.

Oswald went to bed early that festive night, and she sat up thinking about Russia and her friends there.

"It was very depressing, especially when I thought of my home, my relatives who were making merry and I was not with them, but sitting alone and unhappy."

Marina writes of her meeting with Ruth Paine at a mutual friend's house, and of the friendship that grew between them. A short time later, Marina says, Oswald made the attempt to kill Walker, and a few days after that, Oswald told her he had lost his job. "God," she says, "one more misfortune on my head."

Oswald and Marina, who by this time was pregnant with their second child, moved to New Orleans, which Marina liked at first but then came to despise. ". . . . The mosquitoes are terribly vicious," she says, adding, "I could not stand the humid and hot weather."

There Oswald became involved in pro-Castro activities. "He started to spread pro-Cuban leaflets in the city." She writes, "I was not exactly happy with this occupation of his, but it seemed to me better than his 'games' with the rifle as in Dallas. To tell the truth, I sympathized with Cuba. I have a good opinion of this new Cuba, since when I was living in Russia I saw a lot of excellent movies about the new life in Cuba .... But I did not support Lee since I felt that he was too small a person to take so much on himself .... Cuba will get along by itself, without Lee Oswald's help.

"I thought it was better for him to take care of his family. Lee and I quarreled about this, especially one day when he was arrested and spent the night in jail."

Marina writes that Oswald had suggested before they moved to New Orleans that she return to Russia. After his arrest in New Orleans, she says, he began to "think more and more about returning to Russia" himself.

But Marina moved in with Ruth Paine in Irving instead. After an exchange of letters in which Marina described her problems to Mrs. Paine, the suburban housewife, who was having marital difficulties of her own, drove to New Orleans, picked Marina and June up, and took them back to her home. Oswald remained in New Orleans for two weeks, made a brief trip to Mexico City, then moved to Dallas. He found a room in Oak Cliff, and through Mrs. Paine, he got a job as an order filler at the Texas School Book Depository.

On October 18, Oswald celebrated his 24th birthday at Mrs. Paine's house. "Lee was in a very good mood, since he had a job and was expecting a son," Marina says. "He stayed with us through the weekend, and on Sunday, the 20th, in the evening, our daughter was born. Lee stayed at Ruth Paine's on Monday, since June was quieter when her father was there. Monday Lee visited me in the hospital. He was very happy at the birth of another daughter and even wept a little."

On November 22, after Oswald had left the Paine

house, Marina spent the morning watching television "in a very joyful and friendly mood seeing how happy the people were to greet the President." Ruth Paine had taken her children to a doctor that morning, and when she got home, she joined Marina in front of the television set.

Suddenly, the word flashed on the screen that President Kennedy had been shot.

"We were both terribly upset and waited impatiently for news of Kennedy's condition," Marina says. Since her English was poor, Ruth Paine translated the bulletins for her, and informed her that Kennedy had died.

"I was so shocked by this that I wept freely," Marina writes. "I do not know why but I cried for the President as though I had lost a close friend, although I am from a completely different country and know little about him. But all that I knew about him was good.

"I was very sorry for Jacqueline and her children. And I asked myself why fate was so cruel; why good people leave this world so early while some bad ones have the luck to live for a long time.

"Then Ruth said that the shot had come from the building where Lee worked. My heart missed a beat and I thought did my 'crazy' husband do this?

"But the news reports were all different. In the beginning, no one knew who had done it. Everything was mixed up.

"I went into the garage where Lee kept all our things to see if his rifle was in place. But the rifle which was wrapped in a blanket was there. I began to breathe easier, but nonetheless I could not quite come to myself.

"Then all of a sudden, some policemen came and began to search. They asked if Lee had a rifle. I answered that he had. But when they went into the garage and picked up the blanket, the rifle was not there. When I looked I saw this blanket, which lay in its usual position as though there was something inside it. I had seen this rifle three weeks earlier when I became curious as to what was lying there wrapped up in a blanket; I thought that it was some metal pieces of June's bed. I had picked up the edges of the blanket and seen the rifle stock.

"But when it turned out that the rifle was not there, I did not know what to think."

Marina says here that although "99 percent of the evidence was against my husband," she still thought he was innocent.

She was told of her husband's death by Secret Service agents, she writes. On Sunday, November 24, Marina, who had visited Oswald in jail the day before, asked to see her husband again.

"Some Secret Service agents were with us. They said that that morning, when Lee was being taken to another prison, someone had shot him, and then I learned that my husband had died.

"It was a great sorrow for me to be left with two little babies, not knowing English, and without any money.

"But I thought that if my husband actually did this deed, God judged correctly. After all, it is easier to die unexpectedly than on the electric chair under present law."

Throughout her testimony to the Warren Commission, Marina was treated with remarkable courtesy and consideration. One writer described Earl Warren's manner with her as "grandfatherly." He was solicitous of her comfort, gentle in the questioning. At one point, when J. Lee Rankin, the Commission's chief counsel, asked Marina if Oswald owned a rifle or a shotgun in Russia, Marina replied: "I don't know the difference. One and the other shoots. You men. That is your business."

Warren broke into the questioning to assure Marina that "my wife wouldn't know the difference, so it is all right."

Marina spoke freely about Oswald's ownership of a rifle in the United States. She told the Commission she first saw Oswald's rifle in February of 1963, and she said that after that it was "always either in a corner, standing up in a corner, or on a shelf."

"He would hang a coat or something to mask its

presence in the room," she said. "And sometimes when he walked out, when he went out in the evening I didn't know, because I didn't go into that room very often. I don't know whether he took it with him or not."

When Rankin asked her whether she had ever seen Oswald cleaning the rifle, Marina said she thought she had, and she added:

"I think you understand. I want to help you, and that is why there is no reason for concealing anything. I will not be charged with anything."

This is an interesting remark. During her long interrogation and briefing by the Secret Service prior to her appearance before the Warren Commission, a decision obviously was made to grant Marina full immunity from prosecution on any charge that might have grown out of her testimony. She came before the Commission with assurances that she would not face criminal prosecution of any kind.

While comforted by her immunity from possible prosecution, Marina was disturbed by the pressures she claimed the FBI exerted to force her to cooperate with its investigation.

Discussing her interrogation after the assassination, she said:

"In the police station, there was a routine regular questioning, as always happens. (How she knew her questioning was routine, we are not told.) And then after I was with the agents of the Secret Service and the FBI, they asked me many questions of course—many questions. Sometimes the FBI agents asked me questions which had no bearing or relationship, and if I didn't want to answer, they told me that if I wanted to live in this country, I would have to help in this matter, even though they were often irrelevant. That is the FBI."

Rankin displayed some irritation at this comment. "Do you know who said that to you?" he asked Marina.

"Mr. Heitman and Bogoslav, who was an interpreter for the FBI," she said.

Rankin assured her that she was "not under any compulsion to tell the Commission here in order to be able to stay in the country," but Marina repeated her assertion that she was intimidated by the FBI.

"I think that the FBI agents knew that I was afraid that after everything that had happened, I could not remain to live in this country, and they somewhat exploited that for their own purposes, in a very polite form, so that you could not say anything after that. They cannot be accused of anything. They approached it in a very clever, contrived way."

How far did this pressure go toward convincing Marina that her husband was guilty?

She does not tell us. She says that at first she believed her husband was innocent, but "perhaps a week after it all happened, perhaps a little more," she became persuaded that Oswald had killed the President. "The more facts came out, the more convinced I was," she said.

Yet at another point in her testimony, she told a different story. This was when she described her only meeting with Oswald after the assassination. She said that when she spoke to her husband at police headquarters on Nov. 23, she did not ask him if he was guilty of the President's murder or the slaying of Tippit.

"I said, 'I don't believe that you did that, and everything will turn out well,'" Marina recalled. "After all, I couldn't accuse him—after all, he was my husband."

Oswald told her she "should not worry, that everything would turn out well," Marina said. Then she added: "But I could see by his eyes that he was guilty."

When Rankin reminded her that "in the interviews, after the assassination, you first said that you thought your husband didn't do it," Marina replied: "I don't remember it, but quite possibly I did say that."

Her story is full of contradictions. Marina first told the FBI or the Secret Service she believed her husband innocent. Then she told the Commission she became convinced he was guilty about a week after the assassination. But she promptly admits that she really became convinced by looking into his eyes the day after President Kennedy was killed. And when she was asked if she didn't assert his innocence after this visit with Oswald in the police station, she said she did not remember and added: "You must remember that now I only speak the truth."

Marina Oswald was the first and last witness heard by the Warren Commission. She testified first on Feb. 3, 1964, in Washington, again in June, and finally on Sept. 6 in Dallas. During the period between her first two appearances, she provided the Commission with a new touch. She said her husband had plotted to assassinate not only General Walker but Richard M. Nixon, the former vice president, as well.

Marina had told the story of the Nixon plot to Oswald's brother, Robert, who had reported it to the Warren Commission. "In January, 1964," the Commission said, "Marina Oswald and her business manager, James Martin, told Robert Oswald, Lee Harvey Oswald's brother, that Oswald once threatened to shoot former Vice President Richard M. Nixon. When Marina Oswald testified before the Commission on Feb. 3-6, 1964, she had failed to mention the incident when she was asked whether Oswald had ever expressed any hostility toward any official of the United States. The Commission first learned of this incident when Robert Oswald related it to FBI agents on Feb. 19, 1964, and to the Commission on Feb. 21."

On June 11, Marina reappeared before the Commission and gave this account:

Some time in April, 1963—probably around April 20—Oswald put on a good suit, got his pistol and started to leave the house. "I asked him where he was going," Marina said, "and why he was getting dressed. He answered, 'Nixon is coming. I want to go and have a look.'

"I said, 'I know how you look,' or rather 'I know how you customarily look, how you customarily take a look,' because I saw he was taking the pistol with him, rather than I know how you look in the sense that you are dressed; how you look at things is what I mean."

Marina said she was convinced her husband was planning to kill Nixon.

"First I didnt know what to do," she said. "I wanted to prevent him from going out .... I called him into the bathroom and then I started to cry. And I told him that he shouldn't do this, that he had promised me."

She explained that after the Walker shooting, she had elicited from Oswald a promise that he would never try anything like that again.

"I remember I held him," Marina said. "We actually struggled for several minutes, and then he quieted down. I remember that I told him that if he goes out, it would be better for him to kill me than to go out."

Finally, she said, Oswald relented. "He took off his suit and stayed home all day reading a book. He gave me the pistol and I hid it under the mattress."

The story is without much basis in fact, as the Warren Commission itself notes. It is a piece of incriminating information volunteered by Oswald's wife. It seems to have no apparent purpose other than to damage his name further.

The Commission says that no Dallas newspaper mentioned any proposed visit to that city by Nixon between Jan. 1, 1963, and May 15, 1963. Nixon himself told the Commission his only visit to Dallas during 1963 took place on Nov. 20 and 21, the two days before the assassination.

Therefore, the Commission concludes, "regardless of what Oswald may have said to his wife, he was not actually planning to shoot Mr. Nixon at that time in Dallas."

The Commission asked Marina whether Oswald might actually have intended to kill not Nixon but Vice President Lyndon Johnson. He was in Dallas on April 23— three days after the purported incident occurred.

"Yes, no," Marina answered. "I am getting a little confused with so many questions. I was absolutely convinced it was Nixon and now after all these questions, I wonder if I am right in my mind."

Marina's account of the Walker incident does her husband no good either. On the basis of this story, which the Commission had heard from no other source, it concluded that Oswald had a "capacity for violence."

Marina told the Commission how Oswald one day had asked her to take pictures of him with his rifle and revolver, and to keep one of the photographs for his daughter. About two or three weeks later, Marina said, Oswald went out one evening.

"I thought that he had gone to his classes," Marina said, for Oswald then was taking an evening typing course, "or perhaps that he just walked out or went out on his own business. It got to be about 10 or 10:30, he wasn't home yet, and I began to be worried. Perhaps even later.

"Then I went into his room. Somehow, I was drawn into it—you know—I was pacing around. Then I saw a note there . . . On the note it said, 'If I am arrested,' and there are certain other questions such as, for example, the key to the mailbox is in such and such a place, and that he left me some money to last me for some time, and I couldn't understand at all what can he be arrested for.

"When he came back I asked him what had happened. He was very pale. I don't remember the exact time, but it was very late.

"And he told me not to ask him any questions. He only told me that he had shot at General Walker.

"Of course I didn't sleep all night. I thought that any minute now the police will come. Of course I wanted to ask him a great deal. But in his state, I decided I had best leave him alone—it would be purposeless to question him. . . .

"Of course in the morning I told him that I was worried, and that we can have a lot of trouble, and I asked him, 'Where is the rifle? What did you do with it?' "

Oswald told her he had buried it, and he explained that he had shot at Walker because of his political beliefs.

Marina related this incriminating story with little

prompting and with no reluctance. She was the only witness to appear before the Commission and link Oswald with a previous shooting.

Her renunciation of her husband began long before the assassination. It reached a dramatic peak the night before the murder and it continued throughout her testimony to the Warren Commission.

For Oswald, the act of renunciation was much simpler and more eloquent. When he walked out of the Paine house on the morning of Nov. 22, 1963, heading for a rendezvous with history, he left behind his wedding ring. It was the first time in his marriage that he had ever done so.

Oswald left the ring out of despair and as a gesture of renunciation. A few hours later, Jacqueline Kennedy slipped her wedding ring from her finger and placed it in the hand of her dead husband for very different reasons.

Chapter Nine

Why Did Ruby Shoot Oswald?

The murder of Lee Oswald on November 24, 1963, turned the tragedy of Kennedy's assassination into a nightmare.

Most Americans were prepared up to that moment to believe that Oswald was a deranged killer who had somehow, against overwhelming odds, accomplished his ugly objective. But sitting in our living rooms that Sunday morning and watching a stocky little man dart into camera range and kill, we began to doubt. Our doubts never have been entirely resolved.

The Warren Commission tells us much about Jack Ruby's life and hard times. It bombards us with details about Jack Ruby the boy, growing up on the slum streets of Chicago, living in a home torn apart by alcoholism and insanity. It tells us of Ruby's shady incursions into the business world, of his minor brushes with the law, of his concern about his receding hairline and his expanding waistline. It even gives us a glimpse or two of Ruby's sex life.

It parades before us a column of witnesses who describe Ruby as vicious enough to beat drunks nearly to death, yet gentle enough to love dogs, shun violence and offer financial aid to casual acquaintances in need of help. It depicts Ruby as a man who had close associations with underworld figures most of his life, but had no connection with organized crime.

The idea, apparently, is to convince us by this Niagara of detail that Ruby couldn't have been involved in any conspiracy either to kill President Kennedy or to murder his assassin.

The one thing the Warren Commission does not tell us is the one thing we would most like to know about Jack Ruby: Why did he kill Lee Oswald?

The Commission sidesteps this question on grounds of high principle. Ruby was still involved in legal action to escape the Texas electric chair when the Warren Report was published, and the Commission scrupulously sought to avoid any conclusions that might prejudice his defense which was based on the contention that he was insane.

In a brief apologia introducing a section of the Report dealing with Jack Ruby's life, the Commission explains:

"The Commission's desire not to interfere in the pending proceedings involving Ruby necessarily limits the scope of this appendix, which does not purport to discuss the legal issues raised during Ruby's trial or his possible motive for shooting Oswald."

This, of course, is a serious omission. Why Ruby shot Oswald, after all, is one of the essential questions we have a right to ask about the assassination. The answer, which will not be found anywhere in the Warren Report, could influence much of our thinking about the assassination itself.

Instead of being given an answer to this question, we are assured by the Commission that Ruby, like Oswald, acted entirely alone; as in Oswald's case, we are left by the Commission to make the proper inference—that Ruby, like Oswald, had some incomprehensible motive for his crime.

Most of us, however, feel uneasy in the presence of such inferential situations. If the Commission had determined a motive for the murder of Oswald, just as it had determined a motive for the assassination of President Kennedy, might not its conclusions that Ruby and Oswald each acted alone have come under serious question?

To engage for a moment in sheer speculation, suppose Ruby had a more understandable reason for killing Oswald than the reason he gave, which was his desire to spare Mrs. Kennedy the ordeal of testifying at Oswald's trial. Suppose he killed Oswald to prevent him from revealing what he knew about the assassination. Certainly, in the face of a national tragedy of such dimension, this question must be asked and pursued.

But Oswald was locked away in a jail cell, safe from attack. If his murder were to be accomplished quickly, it would have to be done on Sunday morning during his transfer from the Dallas Police Headquarters to the County Jail. Only then would he be exposed, however briefly, to a killer's pistol.

The chronology of Oswald's murder is interesting. No precise time was set for the transfer. Police Chief Curry told reporters the night before that Oswald would be moved around 10 a.m. Sunday. In fact, Oswald was not moved until 11:20 a.m.

Ruby told the Warren Commission he decided on Sunday morning to kill Oswald. Others have asserted that Ruby admitted after the killing that he had begun planning the slaying of Oswald as early as Friday night. Regardless of when Ruby actually decided to commit the murder, by the time he had left his house on Sunday morning, he had made up his mind. He normally carried a gun in the trunk of his car to protect the money he stowed there. But that Sunday morning, he put the gun in his pocket when he left his apartment.

Yet unlike the reporters covering the story of Oswald's transfer, who arrived at the jail before 10 a.m., Ruby did not hurry downtown. He left home shortly before 11 a.m., apparently confident that he would reach Police Headquarters in time for a shot at Oswald. How did he know that he had time to leave home around 11 a.m. when reporters who were in close touch with

Dallas authorities were under the impression that Oswald would be moved at about 10 a.m.?

While last-minute preparations were in progress for Oswald's transfer, Ruby drove downtown, parked his car across the street from a Western Union office a block from Police Headquarters, deposited his billfold containing all of his personal identification in the trunk of his car, and walked over to the Western Union office.

There he sent a $25 money order to an employee who had asked him for an advance on her salary. The Western Union clerk stamped Ruby's receipt 11:17 a.m.

At that moment, Oswald was being moved from Captain Fritz's office to the basement jail office at Police Headquarters.

The Western Union clerk recalled that, after sending the money order, Ruby walked outside and headed directly toward Police Headquarters. He must have gotten there some time around 11:18 or 11:19.

Oswald was brought from the jail office into the basement at 11:20. He was shot at 11:21.

In other words, Ruby reached his target at precisely the right moment. The timing was perfect beyond belief. At exactly the moment that Oswald was vulnerable to attack, Ruby reached him and shot him.

Such precision is difficult indeed to see as coincidence.

If Ruby had arrived at the jail at 10 o'clock, when the reporters assembled there, he would have had to wait an hour and 20 minutes for a shot at Oswald, thus running the risk that his unauthorized presence in the police station might have been discovered before Oswald appeared. If Ruby had left home a few minutes later than he did, or if he had spent an extra minute or two at the Western Union office, he would have missed Oswald entirely. But Ruby committed none of these missteps. He moved with certainty and precision, and reached his goal exactly at the opportune moment.

Could Ruby have plotted this execution without help?

Ruby himself suggested this to the Warren Commission. At one point in his meandering testimony before the Commission, he said of the careful timing of the Oswald murder: "If it were timed that way, then someone in the police department is guilty of giving this information as to when Lee Oswald was coming down."

Ruby was acquainted with many Dallas cops. The Warren Commission quotes Chief Curry as saying that Ruby knew "no more than 25 to 50 of Dallas' almost 1,200 policemen," then notes that "the reports of present and past members of the Dallas Police Department as well as Ruby's employees and acquaintances indicate that Ruby's police friendships were far more widespread than those of the average citizen."

The Commission adds, however, that "there is no credible evidence that Ruby sought special favors from police officers or attempted to bribe them. Although there is considerable evidence that Ruby gave policemen reduced rates, declined to exact any cover charge from them, and gave them free coffee and soft drinks, this hospitality was not unusual for a Dallas nightclub operator. Ruby's personal attachment to police officers is demonstrated by reports that he attended the funeral of at least one policeman killed in action and staged a benefit performance for the widow of another. Ruby regarded several officers as personal friends, and others had worked for him. Finally, at least one policeman regularly dated, and eventually married, one of the Carousel's strippers."

Ruby, the Warren Commission would have us believe, was so kind to policemen purely out of the goodness of his heart and not at all because he "sought special favors" from them.

Jack Ruby's childhood, like Lee Oswald's, was turbulent. Ruby, whose real name was Jacob Rubenstein, was born in 1911 in Chicago. His father, a carpenter, and his mother, an illiterate and slovenly housewife, had immigrated to the United States from a rural area of Poland.

Ruby grew up in a succession of ghetto-like neighborhoods where he learned about the ethnic hatred that seethes in America's cities and where he became sensitive about his Jewish heritage. If life on the streets was unbearable, life in Ruby's home was worse. His father was a heavy drinker frequently arrested for disorderly conduct and assault. His mother was subject to uncontrollable rages. For most of the years of Jack Ruby's childhood, his father and mother fought viciously.

At 11 years of age, Ruby was branded a truant and an incorrigible and referred by the Jewish Social Service Bureau to the Institute for Juvenile Research, which recommended that he, his two younger brothers and a sister be placed in foster homes. The Institute found Ruby "quick tempered" and "disobedient," and concluded that his mother was "thoroughly inadequate in the further training of the boy."

At about this time, Ruby's mother, who was described by one of her daughters as a "selfish, jealous, disagreeable" woman who "never cared to do anything in the home but lie around and sleep," developed a crippling delusional condition. She became convinced that a fishbone was lodged in her throat. Finally, in 1937, she was committed to Elgin State Hospital near Chicago. She was released after three months of treatment, but was reccommitted in 1938 for another short stay. She died in 1944. Ruby's father died in 1958 at the age of 87.

Ruby's education was scant. The records are vague, but the Warren Commission tells us it appears likely that he completed the eighth grade and no more.

From the moment Ruby left school, he plunged into the nether world of the Chicago slums. He scalped tickets for sporting events, sold sports novelty items, associated with lesser sports figures and hoodlums.

In 1933, Ruby and some friends went to the West Coast, where he sold handicapper's tip sheets and worked as a singing waiter. While there, he met Virginia Belasco, the granddaughter of the celebrated playwright and actor, David Belasco, and they went out together occasionally.

Ruby remained on the Coast for four years, then returned to Chicago and became involved in the management of a labor union. A friend, Leon Cooke, was financial secretary of Local 20467 of the Scrap Iron and Junk Handlers Union, and Ruby was hired as an organizer. But two years later, Cooke was shot and killed by the president of the union, who was subsequently acquitted of the murder on grounds that he shot Cooke in self defense. Ruby severed his ties with the union soon after Cooke's death.

In 1943, after working at an assortment of jobs—selling punchboards, busts of Franklin D. Roosevelt and "Remember Pearl Harbor" plaques—Ruby was drafted into the Army Air Force. He spent five weeks at Farmingdale, in Long Island, and the rest of his service time in bases in the South. He was discharged with the rank of private first class in February, 1946.

In 1947, Ruby's sister, Eva Grant, opened a nightclub in Dallas called the Singapore Supper Club, and Ruby joined her there to help run it. He quickly fell in with an array of underworld characters. One of Eva Grant's friends in Dallas was a man named Paul Roland Jones, who at about the time Eva Grant met him had just been convicted of attempting to bribe the sheriff of Dallas. A few months later, Jones was convicted of a Federal narcotics charge.

"During the two years in which Jones was appealing his conviction," the Commission says, "he and other criminals frequented the Singapore Club, then operated by Jack Ruby."

Another friend and sometime partner of Ruby's was a man named Joe Bonds. In 1954, Bonds was convicted of sodomy and sentenced to an eight-year penitentiary term. Much of Ruby's social life, it would seem, focused on criminals and policemen.

Between 1947 and 1959, Ruby moved in and out of various nightclub enterprises in Dallas. None of them did well. In 1953, he gained control of the Vegas Club and in 1959, he obtained the Sovereign Club, which a year later he renamed the Carousel. At the time he murdered Oswald, he was still operating the Carousel and the Vegas as raunchy strip joints.

Jack Ruby was at the offices of the Dallas Morning News placing an ad for his nightclubs when he learned that Kennedy had been shot. He seemed to react violently to the news. One of the newspaper's employees said Ruby was "obviously shaken and an ashen color—just very pale . . . . with a dazed expression in his eyes."

From this moment until he shot Oswald, Ruby almost never relaxed. In a frenetic fever, he darted frantically around the city, punctuating his movements with barrages of local and long-distance phone calls. He called relatives and friends in Dallas, relatives in Chicago, even a childhood friend in Los Angeles. He wept uncontrollably at times, but at other times he regained his composure enough to demonstrate an exercising device he had invented and to buy a large supply of sandwiches for the hard-working policemen of Dallas.

Ruby made one interesting comment while at the Dallas Morning News. "John," he said to an acquaintance there shortly after learning Mr. Kennedy was dead, "I will have to leave Dallas."

During his appearance before the Warren Commission, Ruby explained the comment this way:

"I don't know why I said that, but it is a funny reaction that you feel; the city is terribly let down by the tragedy that happened."

The Warren Commission says that when Ruby left the Dallas Morning News some time before 1:30 on the afternoon of Nov. 22, he went to the Carousel Club. As we have seen, there is an element of disagreement here, since Seth Kantor, the Scripps-Howard reporter, testified that he saw Jack at Parkland Hospital at about 1:30 that day.

Whether Ruby was at the hospital or not, eventually he went to his club, then to his sister's house, then back to the club, then to a delicatessen where he bought $10 worth of food for his sister, then back to her house, where he ate, became sick to his stomach, rested briefly, then resumed his frantic movements.

When he left Eva Grant's house for the second time that day, Ruby "looked pretty bad," she said. "This I remember. I can't explain it to you. He looked too broken, a broken man already. He did make the remark, he said, 'I never felt so bad in my life, even when Ma or Pa died.'"

Still keeping up his rapid phone calls, Ruby went to his apartment, then to a synagogue, where he arrived shortly before the end of a two-hour service that had started at 8 p.m. The rabbi, Hillel Silverman, recalled being surprised that Ruby, though appearing distressed, spoke only about his sister's recent illness, and said nothing about the assassination.

Ruby remained at the synagogue long enough to sip a little punch, then took off again. This time, he headed for Dallas' nightclub belt to check on whether other clubs in town had closed as his had in honor of the President's memory. While driving, he heard a radio broadcast that described how hard the Dallas police were working that night. So he drove to a delicatessen, bought eight sandwiches and 10 bottles of soft drinks, and called Police Headquarters. But he was told the cops had eaten, so he decided to take the sandwiches to the employees of radio station KLIF. Unable to reach anyone at the station by phone, Ruby headed downtown toward Police Headquarters.

Again he drove past a few nightclubs "to see if they were activating," as he put it. At about 11:30 p.m., he reached the police station.

For the first time since the assassination, Ruby moved into close proximity with Lee Oswald. In view of what happened the next time he saw Oswald at the police station, one wonders whether his intentions that night were as innocent as he alleges they were.

Ruby said he got into the building housing the Police Department with little trouble. "I drove down to Commerce and Harwood and parked my car with my dog—

incidentally, I always have my dog with me—on the lot there, left the sandwiches in the car, went into the building of the police station, took the elevator up to the second floor and there was a police officer there," Ruby told the Warren Commission. "The officer was there, and I said, 'Where is Joe Long?'" Long was a KLIF employee Ruby knew of.

"I said, 'Can I go and look for him?'

"Evidently I took a little domineering part about me, and was able to be admitted. I asked different reporters and various personalities there, 'Are you Joe Long?' and I couldn't locate him. I even had a police officer try to page him and he couldn't locate him.

"I recognized a couple of police officers, Cal Jones and a few others, and I said hello to them. And I am still looking for Joe Long but I am carried away with the excitement of history.

"And one fellow then—I am in the hallway there—there is a narrow hallway and I don't recall if Captain Fritz or Chief Curry brings the prisoner out, and I am standing two or three feet away from him, and there is some reporters that did not know the various police officers, and I don't know whether they asked me or I volunteered to tell them, because I knew they were looking to find out who that was, and I said, 'That was Chief Curry' or 'That is Captain Fritz,' or whoever it was."

Because of the jam of reporters and television equipment, the authorities decided to hold their press conference in a larger assembly room in the basement. Everyone moved down there—including Jack Ruby.

"I went down to the assembly room down in the basement," Ruby said. "I felt perfectly free walking in there. No one asked me or anything. I got up on a little table there where I knew I wasn't blocking anyone's view because there was an abutment sticking out and I had my back to the abutment, and I was standing there. Then they brought the prisoner out and various questions were being shouted."

Ruby recalled that District Attorney Henry Wade,

who conducted this celebrated press conference, "let the reporters know that this was the guilty one that committed the crime."

"He specifically stated that in that room, that he was the one," Ruby said. "It didn't have any effect in my mind, because whether the person had come out, whether he come out openly and publicly stated didn't have any bearing in my mind, because I wasn't interested in anything. All I knew, they had the prisoner. But the reporters like to know where they stand, 'is he the one?' "

After the press conference ended, Ruby again tried to reach KLIF by phone. When he finally got through, he arranged for a newsman at the station to tape an interview with District Attorney Henry Wade, and for another KLIF man at the scene to talk to Wade in person. Ruby then left Police Headquarters and took his sandwiches to the radio station.

Ruby stayed there until about 2 a.m., then went to the Dallas Times-Herald, where he demonstrated his "twist-board" exercising device to employees in the paper's composing room.

"Considerable merriment developed when one of the women employees at the Times-Herald demonstrated the board," the Warren Commission said, "and Ruby himself put on a demonstration for those assembled."

At about 4:30 Saturday morning, Ruby drove to his apartment, woke his roommate, George Senator, and began discussing the ad placed in the Dallas Morning News. Ruby had expressed irritation about the ad several times earlier in the day, asserting that it was, as the Warren Commission put it, "an effort to discredit the Jews." Ruby also discussed with the sleepy Senator a sign he had seen in Dallas demanding the impeachment of Earl Warren.

In the midst of this conversation, Ruby got another wild idea. He phoned Larry Crafard, an employee, and told Crafard to meet him and Senator at a garage next door to the Carousel Club and to bring a Polaroid camera with him. Ruby, Senator and Crafard drove from the club to the site of the Impeach Earl Warren sign, and at Ruby's instruction, Crafard took three pictures of the sign. Said Senator of this incident:

"When he was looking at the sign and taking pictures of it, and the newspaper ad .... this is where he really wanted to know the whys or why these things had to be out. He is trying to combine these two together, which I did hear him say, 'This is the work of the John Birch Society or the Communist Party or maybe a combination of both.'"

Still going strong, Ruby drove Crafard and Senator to the post office and demanded to know from a clerk there the name of the person who had rented the post-office box listed on the billboard. The clerk refused to provide Ruby with the information, but Ruby examined the mailbox and, according to Senator, was "upset to find it stuffed with mail."

From the post office, the three men went to a coffee shop where Ruby continued to talk about the sign and the ad. Finally, at 6 a.m., after driving Crafard back to the Carousel Club, Ruby called it a day and went to bed.

But he slept only about two hours. Awakened by a phone call from a friend, Ruby watched television for a while, then drove to Dealey Plaza, the scene of the assassination, and after inspecting the site and weeping, he resumed his round of phone calls. A witness who overheard snatches of a few of these calls on Saturday said Ruby commented about the transfer of Oswald the next day and said, "you know I'll be there."

Ruby's activities the rest of that day are uncertain. Some reporters thought they saw him at Police Headquarters again Saturday afternoon. Later in the day, Ruby visited Eva Grant, went to the Carousel Club for a time although it was closed, then stopped at another nightclub that was open. Ruby told the Warren Commission he retired that night at about 1:30 a.m.

On Sunday morning, Ruby got up at 9 or 9:30, watched television and ate breakfast. At 10:19 a.m., the

Warren Commission says, he got a phone call from one of his strippers, Karen Lynn Carlin.

"Jack answered the telephone," she told the Warren Commission. "And I told him who it was, and he said, 'Yea, well,' and I said, 'I have called, Jack, to try to get some money because the rent is due and I need some money for groceries, and you told me to call.'

"And he said, 'How much will you need?' And I said, 'I'll ask my husband,' and then I said, 'about $25.'

"And he said, 'Well, I have to go downtown anyway, so I will send it to you by Western Union.'"

George Senator said that during the morning, Ruby appeared deeply disturbed. "He was even mumbling, which I didn't understand," Senator said. "And right after breakfast, he got dressed. Then after he got dressed, he was pacing the floor from the living room to the bedroom, from the bedroom to the living room, and his lips were going. What he was jabbering I don't know. But he was really pacing. What he was thinking about. . . .

"I would say that he paced back and forth 5 to 10 minutes," Senator added. Finally, the roommate said, Ruby left the house.

"He said, 'George, I am taking the dog down to the club.' That was it, and out he went."

Ruby himself claimed his emotional state was dramatically affected that Sunday morning by a newspaper piece purporting to be a letter to Caroline Kennedy, the President's daughter.

"Someone had written a letter to Caroline," Ruby said. "The most heartbreaking letter. I don't remember the contents . . . . And alongside that letter on the same sheet of paper was a small comment in the newspaper that, I don't know how it was stated, that Mrs. Kennedy may have to come back for the trial of Lee Harvey Oswald. That caused me to go like I did; that caused me to go like I did.

"I don't know, Chief Justice, but I got so carried away. And I remember prior to that thought, there had never been another thought in my mind. I was never malicious toward this person. No one else requested me to do anything. I never spoke to anyone about attempting to do anything. No subversive organization gave me any idea. No underworld person made any effort to contact me. It all happened that Sunday morning.

"The last thing I read was that Mrs. Kennedy may have to come back to Dallas for trial for Lee Harvey Oswald, and I don't know what bug got ahold of me. I don't know what it is, but I am going to tell the truth word for word.... Suddenly the feeling, the emotional feeling came within me that someone owed this debt to our beloved President to save her the ordeal of coming back. I don't know why that came through my mind."

This statement is challenged by Patrick Dean, a police sergeant who spoke to Ruby right after the murder of Oswald. Dean claimed, to the chargin of one of the Warren Commission's lawyers, that Ruby admitted he had decided to kill Oswald as early as Friday night. As we shall see later, this issue caused a bitter battle between the Commission lawyer and Dean.

Ruby said that when he reached Police Headquarters that morning, "there was a crowd already gathered there. And I guess I thought I knew he was going to be moved at 10 o'clock, I don't know. I listened to the radio, and I passed a crowd and it looked—I am repeating myself—and I took it for granted he had already been moved."

Ruby related how he went to the Western Union office, then walked to the police station.

"I didn't sneak in," he said. "I didn't linger there. I didn't crouch or hide behind anyone, unless the television cameras can make it seem that way.

"There was an officer talking—I don't know what rank he had—talking to a Sam Pease in a car parked up on the curb.

"I walked down those few steps, and there was the person that—I wouldn't say I saw red—it was a feeling I had for our beloved President and Mrs. Kennedy, that he was insignificant to what my purpose was.

"I did not mingle with the crowd. There was no one near me when I walked down that ramp . . . .

"I had the gun in my right hip pocket, and impulsively, if that is the correct word here, I saw him, and that is all I can say. And I didn't care what happened to me.

"I think I used the words, 'You killed the President, you rat.' The next thing, I was down on the floor. I said, 'I am Jack Ruby. You all know me.'

"I never used anything malicious, nothing like S.O.B. I never said that I wanted to get three more (shots) off, as they stated.

"The only words, and I was highly emotional; to Ray Ball—he interrogated more than any other person down there—all I believe I said to him was, 'I didn't want Mrs. Kennedy to come back to trial.'"

Ruby's recollection here clashed with the official story reported by the Warren Commission in only one small detail. The Commission said Ruby shot Oswald "without speaking." Ruby said he accompanied his gunshot with the words, "You killed the President, you rat."

Aside from this small discrepancy, the Commission bought Ruby's story down the line. It accepted without question Ruby's explanation of his motive for killing Oswald, and it accepted equally without question Ruby's description of how he accomplished the murder.

When Police Sgt. Dean suggested that Ruby had offered a somewhat different version right after the killing of Oswald, Dean ran into some rough treatment by Burt Griffin, an assistant counsel to the Commission.

Dean told the Commission that he had been questioned for two hours by Griffin when the lawyer decided their conversation should continue unrecorded. "He advised the court reporter that he would be off the record and he could go smoke a cigarette or get a Coke, and he would let him know when he wanted him to get back on the record," Dean said.

"Well," Dean continued, "after the court reporter left, Mr. Griffin started talking to me in a manner of gaining my confidence in that he would help me and that he felt I would probably need some help in the future.

"My not knowing what he was building up to, I asked Mr. Griffin to go ahead and ask me what he was going to ask me. He continued to advise me that he wanted me to listen to what he had to say before he asked me whatever question he was going to ask me. I finally told him that whatever he wanted to ask me he could just ask me, and if I knew, I would tell him the truth or if I didn't know, I would tell him I didn't know."

Dean said Griffin began talking about two reports Dean had filed after the assassination. One dealt with his interview with Jack Ruby right after the Oswald murder, the second covered Dean's activities in the basement at the time of the murder.

"He said there were things in these statements which were not true, and in fact, he said both these statements, he said there were particular things in there that were not true, and I asked him what portions did he consider not true, and then very dogmatically he said that 'Jack Ruby didn't tell you that he entered the basement via the Main Street ramp.'

"And of course I was shocked at this. This is what I testified to, in fact, I was cross-examined on this, and he, Mr. Griffin, further said, 'Jack Ruby did not tell you that he had thought or planned to kill Oswald two nights prior.'

"And he said, 'Your testimony was false, and these reports to your chief of police are false.'"

Dean said he insisted his statements were true and asked Griffin why he was accusing him of giving false testimony, and Griffin replied, according to Dean, that he was not at liberty to discuss his reasons with Dean.

Before recalling the court stenographer and resuming the recorded portion of Dean's interrogation, Griffin told Dean, according to the police sergeant, "I respect you as a witness, I respect you in your profession, but I have offered my help and assistance, and I again will offer you my assistance, and I don't feel you will be subjecting yourself to loss of your job if you will go ahead and tell me the truth about it."

"I again told Mr. Griffin that these were the facts and that I couldn't change them," Dean informed the Warren Commission. "So with that we got back on the record."

The Warren Commission eventually agreed with Dean that Ruby must have entered Police Headquarters through the Main Street ramp, but it never agreed that Ruby had planned the Oswald murder before Sunday morning.

Other witnesses challenged Ruby's description of his entry into the police station.

Roy Vaughn, the Dallas patrolman who was guarding the entrance to the Main Street ramp at the time Ruby must have entered the police building, swore that Ruby never passed his post.

"Nobody passed me," Vaughn told the Warren Commission.

"Now you know of course that Ruby says that's the way he got in," a Commission lawyer reminded Vaughn.

"Yes, I realize that," Vaughn replied.

"What is your opinion about that statement?" the Commission lawyer asked him.

"I don't believe it," Vaughn said.

"You think he got in some other way?" the Commission counsel asked.

"I don't know definitely," Vaughn said, "but I'll say he didn't come in at the ramp. How he got in—that, I don't know, but I know—I don't believe that he came in the ramp."

Vaughn understandably might have been covering up his own failure to guard the ramp entrance. But his testimony is supported by the statements of Rio S. Pierce, a police lieutenant who drove a car up the Main Street ramp at precisely the time Ruby is supposed to have walked down it. Pierce said he had known Jack Ruby for 12 or 13 years and would have had no trouble recognizing Ruby in a crowd. He said that when he drove up the ramp, he saw a cluster of people at the entrance; Jack Ruby was not there.

There are some important contradictions in Ruby's account of the murder.

Ruby said at one point that he made up his mind to kill Oswald on Sunday morning shortly before he left his house. At another point, he said he left the house a few minutes before 11 a.m. And at still another point, he said he was under the impression when he drove downtown that Oswald was to have been moved at about 10 a.m.

How could Ruby have left the house around 11 o'clock planning to kill Oswald during the transfer, and at the same time be under the impression that it was too late for him to get a shot at Oswald in the basement of Police Headquarters? Ruby was overheard to say on the phone, "You know I'll be there." Yet he did not rush downtown in an effort to reach the police station at 10 o'clock, the time reporters believed the transfer would be made.

Ruby further said that when he got downtown and stopped at the Western Union office, he saw a crowd outside Police Headquarters and assumed that Oswald already had been moved. Nevertheless, Ruby unhesitatingly went from the Western Union office to the basement of Police Headquarters and got there just in time to meet Oswald. If Ruby thought Oswald already had been removed from the police station, why did he go there anyway? Why didn't he try to intercept Oswald at the County Jail?

It seems entirely possible that Ruby knew at 11 o'clock as he was driving downtown that he had not missed Oswald. It seems equally possible that Ruby knew at 11:18 or 11:19 when he walked into the police station that Oswald still had not been moved.

As we have seen before, Ruby's testimony is frequently disjointed, rambling, but occasionally spiced with intriguing remarks.

Seemingly unresponsive to any question then put to him, Ruby said of his murder of Oswald: "Who else could have timed it so perfectly by seconds?" and he followed this with another remarkable comment quoted earlier in this chapter: "If it were timed that way, then someone in the Police Department is guilty of giving the information as to when Lee Harvey Oswald was coming down."

Such remarks make one wonder what is buried in Ruby's turgid testimony.

Chapter Ten

Who Was Lee Oswald?

In the hours after the assassination of John F. Kennedy, our imaginations must have conjured a million visions of the monstrous creature who shot the President.

The slender, slightly bald little man with the angry eyes and enigmatic smirk we saw dragged before the television cameras that night hardly fulfilled our expectations.

We were, one suspects, a bit disappointed as we studied Lee Oswald's face in search of some mark of distinction that would isolate him from ourselves. There was none. There never is. We stared in fascination at the face of Adolph Eichmann a few years ago in the same way, and found there the same disappointment. If television has done nothing else for 20th Century man, it has convinced him that when he looks at the face of evil on the screen, he sees only himself.

Oswald's face, like Eichmann's, was plain, innocuous, neither remarkable for its hideousness nor for its beauty. Indeed nothing about Oswald bore witness to the stain that lay upon his soul.

Ruth Paine, the woman with whom Marina Oswald lived at the time of the assassination, spoke of this quality of undetectability during her testimony to the Warren Commission.

"It seems to me important, very important, to the

record," she said, "that we face the fact that this man was not only human but a rather ordinary one in many respects, and who appeared ordinary.

"If we think that this was a man such as we might never meet, a great aberration from the normal, someone who would stand out in a crowd as unusual, then we don't know this man, we have no means of recognizing such a person again in advance of a crime such as he committed.

"The important thing, I feel, and the only protection we have is to realize how human he was though he added to this sudden and great violence...."

Who was this "rather ordinary" man who became so terrifyingly extraordinary on Nov. 22, 1963?

Lee Oswald was born in New Orleans on Oct. 18, 1939, two months after his father, an insurance premium collector, had died of a heart attack. His mother, Marguerite, had borne two other sons, one by a previous marriage that had ended in divorce.

When he was three, Oswald was placed by his mother in an orphan asylum run by the Evangelical Lutheran Church. Ironically, Oswald's brothers, who were also in the home, remember this as a happy time in their otherwise drab childhood. Oswald remained there a year, then was taken by his mother to Dallas, where she married an electrical engineer named Edwin Ekdahl.

The marriage was stormy. Marguerite was a jealous, emotional woman who once took one of her sons and some of his friends to a nearby apartment to confront Ekdahl in the company of a woman wearing only a negligee. In the summer of 1946, Marguerite gathered her three sons together, left her husband and moved to Covington, Louisiana. She returned to Ekdahl that fall, but in 1948, the marriage collapsed completely and she and Ekdahl were divorced.

Oswald's education began promisingly. His marks in the early years of elementary school were good, despite the frequent changes of schools he was forced to make. As he advanced into the upper grades, however, his work got progressively worse. Reading was his best subject; spelling his worst. His IQ was 103, about normal, the first time it was tested. Some years later, it had risen to 118, which put him in the upper level of bright youngsters.

In 1952, Mrs. Oswald took Lee to New York, where her eldest son, John Pic, was living with his wife and baby. At first, Lee and his mother stayed with John and his family in Manhattan. But this arrangement proved impossible. Mrs. Oswald fought frequently with John's wife, and during a climactic argument, Lee struck his mother and threatened his sister-in-law with a pocket knife.

After this quarrel, Mrs. Oswald and Lee moved to the Bronx. Oswald was enrolled in a public school there, but rarely attended. His truancy became such a serious problem that legal action was initiated by the school authorities after an attendance officer found Oswald "beyond the control of his mother insofar as school attendance is concerned."

On April 16, 1953, Lee Oswald was formally declared a truant by the court and remanded to Youth House for three weeks of psychiatric study. As we saw in an earlier chapter, the staff of Youth House found Oswald a troubled and troublesome youngster, but agreed he was not psychotic. Dr. Renatus Hartogs, the institution's chief psychiatrist, recommended that Oswald be placed on probation and that he and his mother be given guidance by one of New York's social service agencies.

But when a probation officer attempted to find an agency that could help Oswald, his efforts were frustrated. He called the Community Service Society, but was told its facilities were already overburdened and it could not handle another case like Oswald's. The Salvation Army said it was unable to provide the kind of treatment Oswald required.

In the fall, when Oswald went back to school, his behavior continued to show signs of deterioration. He fought with other children, evinced little interest in school work and posed serious disciplinary problems for his teachers. Unable to find another solution, the court began to plan for Oswald's commitment to a training institution for delinquent boys. Before such action could be taken, however, Mrs. Oswald and her son left New York and returned to New Orleans.

Oswald completed the eighth and ninth grades in the Louisiana city. About a month after he started the 10th grade, he presented a note to his teacher. He had written the note himself and signed his mother's name to it. It read:

"To whom it may concern,

Becaus we are moving to San Diego in the middle of this month Lee must quit school now. Also, please send by him any papers such as his birth certificate that you may have. Thank you.

Sincirely

Mrs. M. Oswald."

Without checking, the school authorities accepted this note as genuine and permitted Oswald to drop out of school a few days later.

Oswald promptly tried to enlist in the Marine Corps, but was rejected because he was barely sixteen. He worked for the next few months as a messenger and office boy, then moved with his mother to Fort Worth, where he returned to high school briefly, only to drop out again.

Oswald had started reading books on Communism and Marxism when he was about 15. He once said his interest in left-wing literature was kindled by an old lady he had met in New York who had given him pamphlets about the Rosenbergs, a New York couple who were electrocuted for espionage in 1953. In October, 1956, Oswald took his first known political step. He wrote this letter to the Socialist party of America, the most moderate of all left-wing groups:

"Dear Sirs;

I am sixteen years of age and would like more information about your youth League, I would like to know if there is a branch in my area, how to join ect., I am a Marxist and have been studying socialist principles for well over fifteen months I am very interested in your Y.P.S.L."

Fifteen days after writing this letter, Oswald turned 17. Eight days after that, he enlisted in the Marine Corps.

Oswald's military career was not remarkable in any way, except for two minor clashes with Marine Corps authority while he was stationed in Japan. The first occurred when Oswald opened a locker and a .22 caliber pistol fell to the floor and discharged, wounding him in the arm. Oswald, who by this time was a private first class, was court-martialed for illegal possession of a weapon, broken to private, fined $50 in pay and sentenced to 20 days of hard labor. About a year later, he was court-martialed again for pouring a drink on a sergeant during a brawl in a Japanese cafe. This time he was sentenced to 28 days hard labor and fined $55 in pay.

Aside from these scrapes, he performed his work in the Marines well. During basic training at the Marine Corps Recruit Depot in San Diego, California, he was given a series of aptitude tests which showed him "significantly above the Marine Corps average in reading and vocabulary and significantly below the average in tests in arithmetic and pattern analysis."

In March, 1957, after a short stay at Camp Pendleton, Calif., Oswald was transferred to the Naval Air Station at Jacksonville, Florida, where he was given training in radar, map reading and air traffic control. During this period, he was cleared for the handling of confidential material. From Jacksonville, he was sent to Keesler Air Force Base in Biloxi, Mississippi, for further radar training. Upon completion of this course, he was shipped to the Marine Corps Air Station at El Toro, California, and from there to Japan.

Apparently, it was while he was in Japan that he began to think seriously about defecting to the Soviet Union. He started studying Russian and reading Russian-language publications, and he displayed an increasing interest in world affairs and international politics.

In November, 1958, Oswald was returned to the United States and assigned to an air traffic control squadron at El Toro. The following spring, while still in the Marine Corps, Oswald applied for admission to the Albert Schweitzer College, a small liberal arts institution in Switzerland. The application is revealing not so much of what Oswald actually was like at this time as of what he wanted to be like or wanted others to think he was like.

In the application, he said he had a proficiency in Russian equal to about a year's formal training. He claimed he had completed high school by correspondence courses and that his grade average was 85 percent. He listed his special interests as philosophy, psychology, ideology, football, baseball, tennis and stamp collecting. For the future, he said, he was interested in becoming a writer of short stories "on contemporary American life." And he listed his favorite authors as Jack London, Charles Darwin and Norman Vincent Peale!

Asked to explain why he wanted to attend Albert Schweitzer College, he wrote:

"In order to acquire a fuller understanding of that subject which interest me most, Philosophy. To meet with Europeans who can broaden my scope of understanding. To receive formal Education by Instructers of high standing and character. To broaden my knowledge of German and to live in a healty climate and Good moral atmosphere."

Despite the spelling and grammatical errors in the letter, Oswald's application was approved. In June, he sent the college a $25 registration fee and letter saying he was "looking forward to a fine stay."

Oswald was due to be discharged from the Marine Corps in December, and his application for the Swiss college was for the spring term of 1960, suggesting that when he submitted the application he did indeed intend to attend the college. But his plans changed.

In August, 1959, he requested discharge from the Marines in advance of his scheduled separation. He said that his mother had been injured at work and was unable to support herself, and he backed up his request with affidavits from his mother, a lawyer, a doctor and two friends. A few weeks later, Oswald was transferred to reserve status and released from the Corps.

Early in September, Oswald applied for a passport at Santa Ana, California, stating that he planned to leave the United States on September 21, to attend the Albert Schweitzer College and the University of Turku in Finland, and to travel in Cuba, the Dominican Republic, England, France, Germany and Russia. He received his passport six days later.

Stopping briefly in Fort Worth to visit his mother, Oswald went to New Orleans, boarded the freighter Marion Lykes and sailed on September 20 for Le Havre. Before leaving, he wrote this letter to his mother:

"Well, I have booked passage on a ship to Europe. I would of had to sooner or later and I think it's best I go now. Just remember above all else that my values are very different from Robert's or your's. It is difficult to tell you how I feel. Just remember this is what I must do. I did not tell you about my plans because you could hardly be expected to understand."

Oswald reached Le Havre on Oct. 8, took a channel boat to Southampton, went to London and from there flew to Helsinki. In the Finnish capital, Oswald quickly obtained a visa to enter the Soviet Union and crossed the Russian frontier on October 15.

In Moscow, Oswald was greeted by a young Russian girl, Rima Shirokova, who was assigned by the state tourist office as his guide. Although Oswald's visa permitted him to remain in the Soviet Union only six days, he immediately told the tourist guide he planned to remain there permanently. In a diary Oswald kept, he noted that when he told her this she was "flabbergasted" but agreed to do whatever she could to help him.

Soviet authorities were unimpressed, however, with

Oswald's professions of allegiance to the Soviet government and his desires to become a Russian citizen. On October 21, the day after his visa had expired, he was informed that he must leave Moscow within two hours.

Instead of leaving quietly, Oswald cut his wrist in an apparent suicide attempt which he described in cloyingly romantic words in his diary.

"I am shocked!! My dreams!" he wrote. "I have waited for 2 years to be accepted. My fondes dreams are shattered because of a petty offial . . . . I decide to end it. Soak rist in cold water to numb the pain, than slash my leftwrist. Then plaug wrist into bathtum of hot water . . . . . Somewhere, a violin plays, as I wacth my life whirl away. I think to myself 'How easy to Die' and 'A Sweet Death, (to violins) . . . !"

The suicide attempt failed, however. Oswald was found unconscious in his hotel room by Rima Shirokova and taken to a hospital.

"Poor Rimmea stays by my side as interrpator (my Russian is still very bad) far into the night," Oswald wrote in his diary. "I tell her 'Go home' (my mood is bad) but she stays, she is 'my friend.' "

For the first three days of his hospital stay, Oswald was kept in a psychiatric ward. A psychiatrist who examined him found that he was not dangerous to others and could be transferred to the medical section of the hospital. The doctor concluded that Oswald had inflicted the wrist injury on himself "in order to postpone his departure" from the Soviet Union. "He claims he regrets his action," the hospital report stated. "After recovering he intends to return to his homeland."

Once out of the hospital, however, Oswald renewed his efforts to become a Soviet citizen. Still unable to win any encouragement from Soviet authorities, Oswald decided to attempt another dramatic gesture.

On October 31, he walked into the American Embassy in Moscow, dropped his passport on the receptionist's desk and announced that he had come to renounce his American citizenship. A bit flustered, the receptionist ushered Oswald into the office of Richard K. Snyder, the Embassy's second secretary and senior consular official.

Snyder recalls that Oswald appeared "neatly and very presentably dressed," and he remembers that the young expatriate "took charge in a sense of the conversation right from the beginning." Oswald had come prepared and presented Synder with a note which read:

"I Lee Harvey Oswald do herby request that my present citizenship in the United States of america be revoked.

"I have entered the Soviet Union for the express purpose of appling for citizenship in the Soviet Union, through the means of naturalization.

"My request for citizenship is now pending before the Suprem Soviet of the U.S.S.R.

"I take these steps for political reasons. My request for the revoking of my American citizenship is made only after the longest and most serious considerations.

"I affirm that my allegiance is to the Union of Soviet Socialist Republics."

Apparently a wise and patient man, Snyder sat Oswald down and talked to him. Oswald, Snyder recalled, displayed "all the airs of a new sophomore partyliner," and the consul decided to put him off to give him a little more time to reconsider his drastic actions. Snyder told Oswald the formal renunciation could not be accomplished that day because it was a Saturday. He suggested that Oswald return to the Embassy the following Monday to complete the necessary forms. The consul then notified the State Department in Washington that Oswald had sought to renounce his American citizenship, and copies of Synder's message, which included a full account of his conversation with Oswald, were sent to the CIA and the FBI.

In his diary, Oswald noted after his encounter with Snyder:

"I leave Embassy, elated at this showdown, returning to my hotel I feel now my enorgies are not spent in vain.

I'm sure Russians will except me after this sign of my faith in them."

Oswald did not return to the U.S. Embassy on Monday. Instead, the following day, he composed another message which he mailed to the Embassy. It said:

"I, Lee Harvey Oswald, do hereby request that my present United States citizenship be revoked.

"I appeared in person at the consulate office of the United States Embassy, Moscow, on Oct. 31st, for the purpose of signing the formal papers to this effect. This legal right I was refused at that time.

"I wish to protest against this action, and against the conduct of the official of the United States consular service who acted on behalf of the United States government.

"My application, requesting that I be considered for citizenship in the Soviet Union is now pending before the Suprem Soviet of the U.S.S.R. In the event of acceptance, I will request my government to lodge a formal protest regarding this incident."

There is a naive pomposity in this letter that makes it almost amusing. Oswald was irritated by Snyder's well-intentioned delaying tactics, and though not yet even involved in the process of becoming a Soviet citizen, he is already threatening to have the Soviet government— "my government"—lodge a formal protest against the way he was treated by the American official.

The U.S. Embassy was unshaken by Oswald's threat. It informed Oswald that he would have to appear in person to renounce his citizenship.

Learning from newspaper stories of Oswald's efforts to give up his American citizenship, Oswald's mother and brother attempted to reach him by telephone in Moscow. He refused to accept their calls. Robert Oswald finally got in touch with his brother by cablegram, prompting this letter from Oswald in reply:

"Well, what shall we talk about, the weather perhaps? Certainly you do not wish me to speak of my decision to remain in the Soviet Union and apply for citizenship here, since I am afraid you would not be able to comprehend my my reasons. You really dont know anything about me. Do you know for instance that I have waited to do this for well over a year, do you know that I speak a fair amount of Russian which I have been studying for many months.

"I have been told that I will not have to leave the Soviet Union if I do not care to. this than is my decision. I will not leave this country, the Soviet Union, under any conditions. I will never return to the United States which is a country I hate.

"Someday, perhaps soon, and than again perhaps in a few years, I will become a citizen of the Soviet Union, but it is a very legal process, in any event, I will not have to leave the Soviet Union and I will never.

"I received your telegram and was glad to hear from you, only one word bothered me, the word 'mistake.' I assume you mean that I have made a 'mistake' it is not for you to tell me that you cannot understand my reasons for this very action.

"I will not speak to anyone from the United States over the telephone since it may be taped by the Americans.

"If you wish to corespond with me you can write to the below address, but I really don't see what we can take about if you want to send me money, that I can use, but I do not expect to be able to send it back."

As the Warren Commission notes, some of Oswald's comments in this letter were a bit premature. At the time the letter was written, Oswald had not yet received any assurances whatever from the Soviet government that he would be permitted to remain in Russia.

In reply to a subsequent letter from his brother, Oswald wrote that he had always felt an allegiance to the Soviet Union and had gone there "only to find freedom." In this remarkable testament of renunciation, Oswald turned his back on his family and his homeland, declaring:

"Ask me and I will tell you I fight for communism . . . . I will not say your grandchildren will live under communism, look for yourself at history, look at a world map! America is a dieing country, I do not wish to be a part of it, nor do I ever again wish to be used as a tool in its military agressions."

Oswald said he and his "fellow workers and communist's would like to see the present capitalist government of the U.S. overthrown" because it "exploits all its workers" and because in the United States, "art, culture, and the sprit of man are subjected to commercial enterpraising, religion and education are used as a tool to surpress what would otherwise be a population questioning their government's unfair economic system and plans for war."

Replying to comments his brother had made about the advantages of life in the United States, Oswald said:

"So you speak of advantages. Do you think that is why I am here? For personal, material advantages? Happiness is not based on oneself, it does not consist of a small home, or taking and getting. Happiness is taking part in the struggle, where there is no borderline between one's own personal world, and the world in general. I never believed I would find more material advantages at this stage of development in the Soviet Union than I might of had in the U.S.

"I have been a pro-communist for years and yet I have never met a communist, instead I kept silent and observed, and what I observed plus my Marx'ist learning brought me here to the Soviet Union. I have always considered this country to be my own."

Oswald added:

"In the event of war, I would kill any american who put a uniform on in defense of the american government —any american. . . . . In my own mind I have no attachment's of any kind in the U.S. . . . I want to and I shall live a normal happy and peacful life here in the Soviet Union for the rest of my life . . . . my mother and you are (in spite of what the newspapers said) not objects of affection, but only examples of workers in the U.S."

A third letter to Robert Oswald a short time later demanded that he stop writing and concluded:

"I am starting a new life and I do not wish to have anything to do with the old life.

"I hope you and your family will always be in good health."

Despite all these protestations of devotion to the Soviet Union, Oswald never returned to the American Embassy to renounce his U.S. citizenship. On Jan. 4, 1960, he was summoned to the Soviet Passport Office and informed that he could remain in the Soviet Union indefinitely. He was given an identity card as a stateless person—which disappointed him because he had hoped to secure Soviet citizenship—and sent to Minsk, where nine days later he started work as a metal worker in a radio and television factory.

Oswald lived surprisingly well in Minsk. His pay on a piecework basis at the factory was between $70 and $90 a month, and he got an additional $70 a month from a government agency known as the Red Cross, which also had provided him with $500 to pay for his journey from Moscow to Minsk. Between his salary and his subsidy from the Red Cross, Oswald's income was about the same as that of the manager of the factory where he worked. He paid only $6 a month for an attractive apartment with a balcony overlooking the Svisloch River.

"I'm living big," Oswald noted in his diary, "and am very satisfied."

During the months that followed, Oswald joined a hunting club, went for drives and picnics in the country, met and fell in love with a fellow worker named Ella German. For a while, it seemed that Oswald indeed had found what he was looking for in the Soviet Union.

But his euphoria lasted only a short time before the disenchantment began. In May, 1960, he wrote that he had begun to "feel uneasy inside" about certain aspects of Soviet life. Later that summer, his malaise increased.

"As my Russian improves I become increasingly concious of just what sort of a siciaty I live in," he wrote.

"Mass gymnastics, complusory afterwork meeting, usually political information meeting. Complusory attendance at lectures and the sending of the entire shop collective (except me) to pick potatoes on a Sunday, at a state collective farm: A 'patroict duty' to bring in the harvest. The opions of the workers (unvoiced) are that its a great pain the neck; they don't seem to be esspicialy enthusiastic about any of the 'collective' duties a natural feeling. I am increasingly aware of the presence, in all things, of Lebizen, shop party secretary, fat, fortyish, and jovial on the outside. He is a no-nonsense party regular."

By January, 1961, only a year after his arrival in Minsk, Oswald was intensely dissatisfied.

"I am stating to reconsider my disire about staying," he wrote in his diary. "The work is drab the money I get has nowhere to be spent. No night clubs or bowling alleys no places of recreation acept the trade union dances I have have had enough."

A short time later Oswald launched his lengthy efforts to return to the United States.

Oswald's personal life was disappointing as well during this period. He had asked Ella German to marry him and she had refused. Oswald, who said he had fallen in love with Ella "the first minute" he saw her, was "stunned" by her rejection of his proposal. A few months later, he met Marina and they were married. The day after their wedding, Oswald wrote in his diary:

"In spite of the fact I married Marina to hurt Ella I found myself in love with Marina." Soon after this entry, Oswald wrote another:

"The trasistion of changing full love from Ella to Marina was very painfull esp. as I saw Ella almost every day at the factory but as the days & weeks went by I adjusted more and more (to) my wife mentaly . . . . She is maddly in love with me from the very start."

(Apparently, Oswald's spelling difficulties were contagious. Twice on a single page of the Warren Report, in the section dealing with Oswald's stay in the Soviet Union, the word diary is spelled dairy.)

After his marriage, Oswald intensified his efforts to return to the United States. He began corresponding with his mother and brother again, and he wrote to Sen. John G. Tower, a conservative Texas Republican, asking for his help in obtaining an exit visa from the Soviet Union. Although only a short time earlier Oswald had threatened to have the Soviet government—"my government"—protest his treatment by a U.S. consular official, he now urged Tower to raise "the question of holding by the Soviet Union of a citizen of the U.S. against his will and expressed desires."

After Oswald's defection, the Navy Department had changed his discharge from the Marine Corps from honorable to undesirable, and Oswald, anticipating his return to the United States, attempted to erase this blot on his record. He wrote to John B. Connally, then Governor of Texas but formerly Secretary of the Navy, protesting the undesirable discharge.

"I wish to call your attention to a case about which you may have personal knowledge since you are a resident of Ft. Worth as I am," he said in the letter.

"In November 1959 an event was well publicated in the Ft. Worth newspapers concerning a person who had gone to the Soviet Union to reside for a short time (much in the same way E. Hemingway resided in Paris.)

"This person in answers to questions put to him by reporteds in Moscow criticized certain facets of american life. The story was blown up into another 'turncoat' sensation, with the result that the Navy department gave this person a belated dishonourable discharge, although he had received an honourable discharge after three years service on Sept. 11, 1959, at El Toro, Marine corps base in California.

"These are the basic facts of my case.

"I have and allways had the full sanction of the U.S. Embassy, Moscow USSR. and hence the U.S. government. In as much as I am returning to the U.S.A. in this year with the aid of the U.S. Embassy, bring with me my family (since I married in the USSR) I shall employ all means to right this gross mistake or injustice to a boni-fied U.S. citizen and ex-serviceman. The U.S. government has no charges or compaints against me. I ask you to look into this case and take the neccessary steps to repair the damage done to me and my family. For information I would direct you to consult the American Embassy, Chikovski St. 19/21, Moscow USSR."

Governor Connally sent the letter to the Navy Department, which refused to reconsider Oswald's discharge status.

Once all the permits and visas had been obtained from the Soviet and U.S. governments, Oswald faced the problem of raising money for the trip home. His mother suggested she collect the necessary funds by telling the newspapers of Oswald's plight and soliciting contributions from the public. Oswald rejected this idea. The U.S. Embassy in Moscow then came up with the proposal that Oswald borrow the money from the State Department. Accordingly, Oswald applied to the Embassy for a loan of $800. The Embassy told him he could have no more than $500 and finally approved a loan of $435.71, just enough to cover passage for Oswald, his wife and their daughter from Moscow to New York. Oswald repaid the loan in full between August, 1962, and January, 1963.

On the ship from Amsterdam to New York, Oswald took a leisurely look backward at his stay in the Soviet Union. He concluded that neither communism nor capitalism provided the social answers he was seeking. "One offers oppression the other poverty," he wrote. "Both offer imperialistic injustice, tinted with two brands of slavery."

A third system was necessary, Oswald decided. Such a system, he wrote, would draw the best from each of the established social systems, but remain "utterly opposed to both systems."

This new system, Oswald said, could best be established after "conflict between the two world systems leaves the country without defense or foundation of government," or when "economic, political or military crisis, internal or external, will bring about the final destruction of the capitalist system."

Oswald proposed that those wishing to replace the old capitalist and communist systems with a new social order should gather "in a special party" that would "safeguard an independent course of action after the debacle."

Oswald made it clear in these shipboard musings that for the moment at least he had lost all faith in communism.

"The Comunist Party of the United States has betrayed itsef!" he wrote. "It has turned itself into the traditional lever of a foreign power to overthrow the government of the United States; not in the name of freedom or high ideals, but in servile conformity to the wishes of the Soviet Union and in anticipation of Soviet Russia's complete domination of the American continent. . . .

"There can be no sympathy for those who have turned the idea of communism into a vill curse to western man.

"The Soviets have committed crimes unsurpassed even by their early day capitalist counterparts, the imprisonment of their own peoples, with mass extermination so typical of Stalin, and the individual surpresstion and regimentation under Krushchev.

"The deportations, the purposefull curtailment of diet in the consumer slighted population of Russia, the murder of history, the prostitution of art and culture."

Reading these confused and immature ramblings, one can see Oswald at a turning point. More politically preoccupied than ever, he is now susceptible to almost any extremist philosophy whether right wing or left wing in orientation.

He seems to be seeking any new social concept that is disassociated from the established forms of East and West. Within this mind in search of grandiose political schemes, there is room for the right-wing extremism so prevalent in Dallas, and there is room as well for the radical left-wing views of the Progressive Labor Movement.

Poorly educated, bereft of critical faculties, without a

firm grasp of any philosophy, yet still completely committed to political salvations, Oswald is open to any persuasion that is new and dramatically different from those systems that have shattered his illusions about life.

In this context, some of Oswald's seemingly contradictory actions become more comprehensible. It becomes entirely conceivable for a man in this state of political confusion to strike at General Walker in April and to assassinate President Kennedy in November. The contradiction no longer appears insurmountable.

Back in the United States, Oswald remained politically dormant for a time. In January of 1963, he bought a Smith & Wesson .38 caliber revolver, the weapon used in the Tippit murder, from a Los Angeles mail-order gun dealer. In March, he purchased the rifle used in the Kennedy assassination from Klein's Sporting Goods, a Chicago mail-order house.

By early March, only about eight months after his return to the United States, Oswald had swung into action again, planning the murder of General Walker. Marina Oswald told the Warren Commission that Oswald took pictures of Walker's house and the surrounding area during the March 9-10 weekend, made notes in preparation for the shooting, and checked bus schedules to plot his escape.

After the unsuccessful attempt on Walker's life, Oswald and Marina moved to New Orleans, where he immediately stepped up his political activities. He organized the New Orleans branch of the Fair Play For Cuba Committee, and distributed leaflets supporting Fidel Castro on the streets of New Orleans. At the same time, he got in touch with Carlos Bringuier, a New Orleans leader of the avidly anti-Castro Cuban Student Directorate, and offered not only to help train Cubans to fight Castro but to join them in battle himself.

Four days after making this offer to Bringuier, who was suspicious of Oswald's motives, Oswald was back on the street distributing his pro-Castro leaflets when Bringuier and two friends spotted him. A fight erupted and Oswald and the three Cuban refugees were arrested.

To the best of anyone's knowledge, Oswald was the sole member of the New Orleans chapter of the Fair Play For Cuba Committee, but his arrest provided him with enough notoriety to bring invitations to appear on a radio debate as the committee's spokesman.

The moderator of the debate, William Stuckey, thought Oswald "a very logical, intelligent fellow" who "handled himself very well" despite the fact that during the debate, Oswald's opponent, who had done some checking on his background, revealed publicly that Oswald had defected to the Soviet Union.

Now Oswald performed another of those characteristic shifts from one strongly held position to its opposite. He wrote to the Communist Party in New York—the group he had so recently denounced for betraying itself—and informed its officers of his activities in New Orleans. He got this letter from Arnold Johnson, director of the party's information and lecture bureau:

"It is good to know that movements in support of fair play for Cuba has (sic) developed in New Orleans as well as in other cities. We do not have any organizational ties with the Committee, and yet there is much material that we issue from time to time that is important for anybody who is concerned about developments in Cuba."

In another exchange of correspondence with Communist officials in New York, Oswald expressed concern about whether public knowledge of his defection might force him to go "underground." Johnson replied that "often it is advisable for some people to remain in the background, not underground."

In late September, 1963, Marina and her daughter left New Orleans for Dallas in the company of Ruth Paine. Two days later, Oswald went to Mexico City, where he hoped to obtain a Cuban visa and go to Havana.

Oswald traveled by bus to Mexico City and remained there for five days. While in the Mexican capital, he visited the Soviet Embassy seeking a visa to enter the Soviet Union again, but was turned down. He also visited the Cuban Embassy, but there too his visa application was rejected.

Frustrated by what he considered inept Cuban officials, Oswald went to Dallas, rented a room and began to search for a job. He had no immediate success. Finally, on October 14, Ruth Paine mentioned Oswald's employment problem to a neighbor whose younger brother worked at the Texas School Book Depository. The neighbor said she thought there was an opening at the depository. Mrs. Paine called the depository superintendent, Roy Truly, who agreed to talk to Oswald if he applied for the job in person.

Next day, Oswald was hired. He began work at the depository as an order filler on October 16. His employment there ended on November 22.

Chapter Eleven

Guilty Or Innocent?

Transcending all other questions about the assassination of John F. Kennedy are these: Does the story presented to the American people by the Warren Commission survive close scrutiny? Does the Commission establish beyond reasonable doubt that Oswald killed President Kennedy? Does it prove that Oswald and Ruby each acted independently of any accomplices?

Unfortunately, the answers to two of these three questions must be negative. Uncertainty continues to hang like a pall over virtually every significant aspect of the assassination.

We are uncertain about Oswald's motives. We are uncertain about how many shots were fired at Mr. Kennedy and about the precise location of his wounds. We are uncertain about what happened when Oswald was arrested and questioned. We are uncertain about how Ruby got into the police station at exactly the right moment to kill Oswald. We are uncertain about Ruby's motive for killing Oswald. We are uncertain about the existence of conspiracies either in the Kennedy assassination or the Oswald murder or in both.

All that remains is a skeleton of certainty: That Oswald participated in the assassination of President Kennedy, either alone or in concert with others; that Oswald killed Tippit, although under precisely what circumstances remains unclear; that Oswald was slain by Ruby. The bones are there, but the flesh is missing.

This then is the Commission's achievement. It proved beyond much doubt half of what it hoped to prove. It showed that Oswald owned a rifle used in the assassination, that he was on the sixth floor of the book depository at the time shots were fired at the President from there, and that he had a rifle with him. It persuaded all but the most die-hard skeptics that no mistake had been made when the Dallas police arrested Oswald as an assassin barely ninety minutes after the President's murder.

But by ignoring testimony that did not fit, by overlooking witnesses, by withholding evidence and leaving dozens of questions unanswered, the Commission failed to prove the other half of its contention: That Oswald and Ruby each acted alone.

To be sure, the Warren Commission's unfulfilled arguments about the absence of conspiracy do not prove that conspiracy existed. Oswald and Ruby might have operated entirely alone, as the Warren Commission would like to convince us they did. The problem is that the Commission, our only authoritative source of information about the assassination thus far, did not provide a sufficient number of answers to a multitude of questions to permit this conclusion to be drawn. When questions are asked and the answers are not given or are given evasively, the possibility arises that the conclusions are erroneous.

Nevertheless, despite the weaknesses which one suspects the Commission itself must have been aware of, the Commission stated this premise as a cautiously worded conclusion and attempted to shore it up with whatever evidence seemed to conform to the pattern it required. The Commission had a duty to comfort the American people about the stability and health of our society in a moment of extreme distress. We emerged from the nightmare of Dallas full of dark fears about ourselves and our society. The Commission patted us on the head, told us our fears were groundless, and assured us that the events we had just witnessed were merely the acts of isolated aberrants.

Time has passed. The Report has been read and studied. The doubts and uncertainties if anything gnaw more persistently.

"Besides telling the American people what they desperately wanted to hear," said Liberation magazine editorially in its March, 1965, issue, ". . . . the Warren Commission turned out a superficially plausible report and 26 volumes of evidence, which since it is much too long for most people to read, let alone assimilate, was at first assumed to back up the Commission's conclusions. Now that the deed has been done. . . .it seems impossible that the Commission could have expected to get away with it in the long run, but the same could be said in retrospect of most of the egregious miscalculations of history.

"One hesitates to speculate whether the Commission found itself trapped and saw no other way out, or whether it was content to perform a mere holding operation, convinced that time was of the essence and that most Americans would judge charitably on the theory that the Commission's actions helped save American prestige and preserve American morale during an emergency. . . .

"In any event, it is already a not very well kept secret that the Warren Report will not stand up to scientific analysis and objective inquiry, and the process of exposing its failings is well under way."

Even if there were no other persuasive reasons for doubting many of the Warren Commission's conclusions, the methods it employed in reaching them would be cause enough.

The Commission was charged at its creation with the responsibility of ascertaining as fully as humanly possible the truth about the murder of the President. To determine such truth, it obviously had to examine every shred of evidence it could find before submitting its verdict to the American people. But as we have seen, it did not consider all the evidence. It overlooked some witnesses, ignored the testimony of others, and withheld even from itself such important items as the X-rays and photographs of President Kennedy's body.

What evidence the Commission did examine was almost exclusively provided by police agencies—the Dallas authorities, the FBI, the Secret Service and the CIA. The Commission had no independent investigators of its own.

"Because of the diligence, cooperation, and facilities of Federal investigative agencies," the Commission explained, "it was unnecessary for the Commission to employ investigators other than the members of the Commission's legal staff."

This created an ominous agglomeration: A body of governmental figures relying for its information on Federal and local police agencies.

It all sounds familiar. In our criminal courts, where a prosecutor normally bases his case on information supplied by the police, a similar structure exists.

There is a striking difference, however, between the positions of the courtroom prosecutor and the Warren Commission. The prosecutor's case is subjected to relentless challenge at every step by a defense lawyer. When the prosecutor puts forth an argument, it is countered by the defense counsel. When the prosecutor elicits damaging testimony from a witness, the defense lawyer has the opportunity to cross-examine that witness or to present witnesses of his own in reply. When the prosecutor submits exhibits to the court, the defense can attack them with evidence of his own.

There was no voice in the Warren Commission's investigation to challenge anything. No evidence was questioned, unless the Warren Commission questioned it. No issues were raised unless the Commission raised them. No testimony was evaluated except by the Commission and its staff. No witnesses were cross-examined by anyone.

The Commission played all the parts in this surprisingly low-key courtroom drama. It was the judge, the jury, the prosecutor and the defense counsel. It played some better than others. The result is a statement that rings with the timbre of a prosecutor's voice. Search as one may, one cannot hear that other voice—the voice of challenge and dissent—anywhere in the Warren Report. It is frightening to consider that, to judge by the Report itself, no member of the Warren Commission took issue or disagreed with a single statement made in that voluminous document. Such unanimity gives the members of the Commission a faceless quality straight out of George Orwell.

The absence of dissent is not a minor lapse on the Commission's part. It goes to the very heart of the question of whether the Commission could possibly hope to learn the truth under the conditions it established for itself. If a dissenting voice had been heard, even faintly the ultimate image of the assassination very likely would have been appreciably different. Questions that remain unanswered might have been answered. Elements that were omitted because they did not fit the Commission's preconceptions about the assassination might have been given their proper weight. Lines of inquiry that were dropped or evaded might have been pursued. The parts might have fitted together into a different whole.

The Commission offers a rather feeble apology for its failure to permit a dissenting voice to be heard. In the preface to its Report, it says:

"The procedures followed by the Commission in developing and assessing evidence necessarily differed from those of a court conducting a criminal trial of a defendant present before it, since under our system there is no provision for a posthumous trial.

"If Oswald had lived, he could have had a trial by American standards of justice where he would have been able to exercise his full rights under the law. A judge and jury would have presumed him innocent until proven guilty beyond a reasonable doubt. He might have fur

nished information which could have affected the course
of his trial. He could have participated in and guided his
defense. There could have been an examination to
determine whether he was sane under prevailing legal
standards. All witnesses, including possibly the defendant, could have been subjected to searching examination under the adversary system of American trials.

"The Commission has functioned neither as a court
presiding over an adversary proceeding nor as a prosecutor determined to prove a case, but as a factfinding
agency committed to ascertainment of the truth."

Why the Commission believed that because Oswald
was dead, it could not permit the "searching examination" of its witnesses is difficult to understand. Such
examination, it would seem, would have enhanced rather
than diminished the likelihood of ascertaining the truth.

The inconsistency of the Commission's reasoning becomes still more apparent when one considers that much
of the evidence presented by the Warren Commission in support of its conclusions would never have
been admitted into the record if Oswald had lived to
stand trial.

As Alfredda Scobey, a member of the Commission staff,
noted in the American Bar Association Journal, the Warren Report is "crammed with facts that would not be
admissible in the trial of a criminal case."

Typical of such inadmissable evidence upon which
the Commission relied so heavily, Miss Scobey says, was
the largely uncorroborated and highly damaging testimony of Oswald's wife, Marina. Miss Scobey says that
Marina provided the Commission not only with many
facts that connected Oswald directly with the assassination, but she also was the sole source of a "wealth of
background information" upon which the Commission
based its assessment of Oswald's character and behavior
in formulating what Miss Scobey calls the "motiveless
motive" for the assassination.

Miss Scobey and others are quick to point out that
while such evidence would not have been admitted if

Oswald were on trial, in reality he was dead and the Warren Commission was not limited by the proscriptions of the courtroom.

This is a curious kind of logic. Because Oswald was dead, it suggests, uncorroborated testimony, which can easily be composed of large helpings of lies and fabrications or might simply be distorted by ignorance, goes unchallenged and is permitted to form the basis of much of the case.

If anything, reason dictates that such normally inadmissible evidence should have been subjected to even more vigorous scrutiny under these circumstances than it might have received in a courtroom.

The structure of a trial, as it evolved under American law, provides an opportunity for a defense lawyer to refute the prosecution's case. This system works not only because it usually protects the rights of the defendant, but also because it aids in discovering the truth. It sifts and screens evidence, stacks it up against contradictory information, highlights inconsistencies and distortions, and exposes lies.

This is not to say that the Commission should have conducted a full-dress, posthumous trial of Lee Oswald. Such a spectacle would have been an empty gesture, since Oswald was dead and the protection of his rights as a defendant had ceased to be of paramount concern. But simply because no trial was held does not mean that the Commission should have abandoned tested methods of determining the truth through the close scrutiny of evidence, the "searching examination" of witnesses, the independent initiative of a dissenting advocate. In rejecting these traditional tools of the law court, forged above all to lead toward the truth, the Commission fell into a mire of haphazard methods that obscured the truth behind a fog of unsubstantiated distortions and outright lies.

Just as one might expect, the Commission itself was uneasy about its methods and its ability to perform its lofty, self-proclaimed duty as a factfinding agency.

Three months after it began its work, it suddenly summoned Walter E. Craig, the president of the American Bar Association, to "participate in the investigation and to advise the Commission whether in his opinion the proceedings conformed to the basic principles of American justice."

In other words, after three months of work, the Commission—composed of seven lawyers including the chief justice of the United States—was dubious about whether it was indeed functioning as a factfinding agency or whether it was building a prosecution case, and it felt the need to call upon an independent legal expert for advice and help.

Craig did not enter the lists like a Clarence Darrow to slay the dragons of distortion. He cross-examined no one, challenged no evidence, asked almost no questions. He was seen in the Commission's chambers. He appointed assistants who performed their work quietly and are not identified in the Warren Report.

Mark Lane, a rather bombastic lawyer, had the right idea but to the Commission was obviously the wrong man. He demanded the Commission's permission to represent Lee Oswald's interests during the investigation. The Commission turned him down.

Its decision probably was the correct one. Lane's participation would not have enhanced the prospects for cool, contemplative inquiry. But Craig and his appointed assistants do not appear to have played devil's advocate in the investigation, so the role went sadly uncast.

What was needed was a responsible, vigorous, independent lawyer who represented not Oswald's interests, but the interests of the American people, as contrasted with the American political establishment.

His purpose would have been to raise the questions the American people wanted answered, to cross-examine witnesses, to produce witnesses of his own, to pursue fruitful lines of inquiry abandoned by the Commission's lawyers, to prevent distortions and evasions from cluttering the Commission's record.

Had he performed his purpose well, the Commissio
could have performed its better. It could have functione
as a genuine factfinding body, listening to the informa
tion obtained by police agencies and to attacks by th
devil's advocate, then determining where the truth lay

Charged with such responsibility, our public inquire
would have spared us a host of uncertainties that remain

He would have insisted, for example, that the Com
mission determine the source of the initial police alarm
for a suspect in the assassination.

Moments after the assassination, the Commission tell
us, Howard Brennan, the pipefitter who was across th
street from the book depository when the motorcade
passed, reported to policemen that he had seen a mar
firing a rifle from the building's sixth floor.

"Within minutes of the assassination, Brennan de
scribed the man to police," the Commission said. "Thi
description most probably led to the alert sent to police
cars at approximately 12:45 p.m."

The Commission leaves us in doubt about a key issue
here. It says Brennan "most probably" was the source of
the information broadcast at 12:45, fifteen minutes after
the shooting. But it is not sure. The reason for the Com
mission's uncertainty? It was unable—or did not bother
—to locate any policemen to whom Brennan had reported
his observations, and it apparently did not ask the police
radio dispatcher where he got the description he broad
cast at 12:45 p.m.

If our public inquirer had been present, he would have
demanded a more precise determination than this of
the source of the dispatcher's information. Had a policeman been found who took the information from Brennan and reported it to the dispatcher, a dark cloud of
doubt would have been dissipated. If it turned out that
no policeman took such information from Brennan, and
that the dispatcher's description came from another
source, an entirely new area of investigation would have
been uncovered.

Such a representative of the public interest would

not have permitted the Warren Commission to suppress the X-rays and photographs of President Kennedy's body. He would have demanded, on our behalf, the right to see such vital evidence and to determine from it the precise location of the President's wounds.

He would have discovered uncalled witnesses like Mr. and Mrs. Frank Wright, whose account of the Tippit murder differed so drastically from the version provided by the police and the Warren Commission.

He would have located the four newspaper employees who heard shots coming from behind them on the grassy knoll to the west of the book depository.

He would have insisted on hearing from more than two witnesses to Oswald's arrest in the movie theater.

He would have questioned Captain Fritz in more detail about his unrecorded interrogations of Oswald, and he would not have allowed the Warren Commission to put Fritz's destruction of important evidence behind evasive language.

He would have probed much more deeply into the so-called "police" car that signaled in front of Oswald's rooming house.

He would have examined more closely the circumstances surrounding Oswald's death.

In short, he would have attempted to clear up the myriad little puzzles that remain unsolved.

Unfortunately, the key words here are "would have." Such an advocate for the people was never appointed. His questions—which are really our questions—remain unanswered.

The Warren Commission deprived us of his counsel, and in doing so, it robbed us of the confidence we should have felt about the results of its investigation. The American people were the losers. We were the ones who, by the inadequacy of the Commission's methods, were denied reasonable certainy about what took place on November 22, 1963.

Chapter Twelve

Can It Happen Again?

On the morning of November 22, 1963, during a brief break in a hectic round of political appearances, President Kennedy sat in a room at the Hotel Texas in Fort Worth, chatting with his wife and his close friend and adviser, Kenneth P. O'Donnell.

The conversation turned casually to the subject of Presidential protection by the the Secret Service.

"He was commenting to his wife on the function of the Secret Service, and his interpretation of their role once the trip had commenced," O'Donnell recalled.

Mr. Kennedy felt that the main purpose of the Secret Service was "to protect him from crowds, and to see that an unruly or sometimes overexcited crowd did not generate into a riot, at which the President of the United States could be injured."

Then, O'Donnell said, President Kennedy made this macabre observation:

"If anybody really wanted to shoot the President of the United States, it was not a very difficult job—all one had to do was get a high building some day with a telescopic rifle and there was nothing anybody could do to defend against such an attempt on the President's life."

A half-hour later, President Kennedy left the hotel and

flew to Dallas. Two hours after that, he died by precisely the method he had described that morning.

John F. Kennedy thus became the fourth American President to fall by an assassin's hand. A gun was the weapon of choice in every case, although Mr. Kennedy's murder was the first in which a rifle was employed.

Abraham Lincoln was the first American President to die by assassination. He was shot by John Wilkes Booth, a well-known actor, on the night of April 14, 1865, while watching a play at Ford's Theater in Washington, and died the next day. Booth, an ardent supporter of the Confederate cause, was shot and killed by Federal troops on April 26, 1865, at Bowling Green, Virginia. Two months later, four of Booth's fellow conspirators were tried and sentenced to death and four others were imprisoned.

James Garfield was the second. He was shot by Charles J. Guiteau, a disgruntled politician, on July 2, 1881, in a Washington railroad station. Garfield died on Sept. 19, 1881. Guiteau, who was captured immediately, was hanged on June 30, 1882.

William McKinley was the third. He was shot on Sept. 6, 1901, by Leon F. Czolgosz, a self-styled anarchist, during a public reception for the President at the Pan American Exposition in Buffalo. McKinley died on Sept. 14, 1901. Czolgosz, who was also captured moments after the shooting. was electrocuted 45 days later.

In addition to the four Presidents who have been assassinated, four others have been the targets of unsuccessful assassination attempts: Andrew Jackson and Harry Truman while they were in office; Theodore Roosevelt while he was campaigning for the Presidency in 1912, and Franklin D. Roosevelt after he had been elected but before his first inauguration.

This adds up to an alarming record, as the Warren Commission points out. Since 1865, one out of every five Presidents has died by assassination. Attempts have been made on the lives of one out of every three.

The Secret Service, which now bears the major responsibility for protecting the President from harm, was born in the year that Lincoln died. A division of the Treasury Department, its initial duty was to combat counterfeiting. Until the last decade of the 19th Century, Presidents were offered little or no formal protection while in office. On the night Lincoln was shot, for instance, he was guarded by a single Washington policeman—who was out having a drink at a nearby saloon when Booth crept into the President's box and fired.

In 1894, while investigating a plot by Colorado gamblers to assassinate President Grover Cleveland, the Secret Service assigned a small detail of men to the White House as a precautionary measure. The agents were removed at Cleveland's request, however, when newspapers opposed to the Administration complained of the Secret Service's presence.

But a precedent had been established. During the Spanish-American War, Secret Service men again were assigned to the White House. This time they stayed. In 1902, shortly after the war ended, the Secret Service undertook formal, full-time protection of the President.

Guarding the President is not an easy job. If anything, it becomes increasingly difficult as improved transportation permits the President to travel about the world more easily and more frequently. To meet these growing complexities, the Secret Service has been enlarged to a force of about 600 men with offices in 65 cities in the United States and abroad, and an annual budget of about $12 million. The White House detail, which originally consisted of two men, has grown to about 40.

Despite this growth, it is painfully obvious that the Secret Service and the much larger and more powerful FBI, which has assumed over the years more and more responsibility for the preventive intelligence work connected with Presidential protection, failed abysmally to safeguard President Kennedy's life.

In the finest and most courageous chapter in its entire

report, the Warren Commission examined in detail the reasons for this failure and offered some corrective recommendations. Without equivocation or evasion, the Commission placed blame for the failure to protect the President squarely where it belonged—on the Secret Service and the FBI.

As we saw earlier, no information about Lee Oswald appeared in the Secret Service's Protective Research Section files. These files contain thousands of pieces of information about potential assassins, but on Nov. 22, 1963, they contained nothing about Lee Oswald, despite the fact that he was well known to the FBI, the State Department and the CIA and that stories about his defection to the Soviet Union and his arrest while distributing pro-Castro leaflets appeared in newspapers and on television. The Commission places the responsibility for this grave omission largely on the shoulders of the FBI.

"The Commission believes. . . .that the FBI took an unduly restrictive view of its responsibilities in preventive intelligence work, prior to the assassination. The Commission appreciates the large volume of cases handled by the FBI (636, 371 investigative matters during fiscal 1963). There were no Secret Service criteria which specifically required the referral of Oswald's case to the Secret Service; nor was there any requirement to report the names of defectors. However, there was much material in the hands of the FBI about Oswald; the knowledge of his defection, his arrogance and hostility to the United States, his pro-Castro tendencies, his lies when interrogated by the FBI, his trip to Mexico where he was in contact with Soviet authorities, his presence in the School Book Depository job and its location along the route of the motorcade. All this does seem to amount to enough to have induced an alert agency, such as the FBI, possessed of this information to list Oswald as a potential threat to the safety of the President."

The Commission added that " a more alert and carefully considered treatment of the Oswald case" by the

FBI would have led to transmission of information about Oswald to the Secret Service. There is little doubt that if the Secret Service had known what the FBI knew about Oswald—capped by the fact that Oswald was employed in a building along the President's motorcade route—it would have taken steps to prevent Oswald from acting as he did.

The Commission was not impressed by the declarations of officials of both the FBI and the Secret Service that the two agencies maintained adequate communication with each other. "The Commission does not believe that the liaison between the FBI and the Secret Service was as effective as it should have been," the Commission said.

The Warren Commission also found what it called "certain shortcomings and lapses" in the Secret Service's advance planning for the President's trip to Dallas.

The most shocking of these was the Secret Service's revelation that it did not check buildings along the motorcade route. Americans had assumed for years that such checks were routinely made by the Secret Service. They were surprised and appalled to learn that, with only a few exceptions, the Secret Service never surveyed buildings for potential assassins or possible points of ambush.

"Except for inauguration or other parades involving foreign dignitaries accompanied by the President in Washington," James J. Rowley, the head of the Secret Service, told the Warren Commission, "it has not been the practice of the Secret Service, to make surveys or checks of buildings along the route of a Presidential motorcade. . . . Building are not checked either by Secret Service agents or by any other law-enforcement officers at the request of the Secret Service."

Rowley asserted that it was "not practical" to check buildings along a motorcade route "with the number of men available to the Secret Service and the time available."

The Warren Commission was firm in rejecting his argument. "This justification of the Secret Service's standing policy is not persuasive," the Commission said. "The danger from a concealed sniper on the Dallas trip was of concern to those who had considered the problem. President Kennedy himself had mentioned it that morning."

While it may not be possible to check every building along a motorcade route, the Commission said, it certainly is possible to scrutinize those posing the greatest risk. "An attempt to cover only the most obvious points of possible ambush along the route in Dallas might well have included the Texas School Book Depository Building."

On Feb. 15, 1965, Rowley's outlook was somewhat changed.

"We have instituted a system of building inspections and greatly increased the number and duties of protective personnel along the President's route," he told a Congressional subcommittee conducting closed hearings on increased budgetary allocations to the Secret Service for Presidential protection.

If the American people were surprised to learn no building checks were made by the Secret Service, they were even more surprised to discover that there was no Federal law making it a crime to murder the President. Oswald could not have been prosecuted under Federal statute as Kennedy's assassin. Had he lived, he would have been tried for murder under Texas law.

"Murder of the President has never been covered by Federal law," the Warren Commission said. "It is anomalous that Congress has legislated in other ways touching upon the safety of the Chief Executive or other Federal officers, without making an attack on the President a crime."

In its recommendations, the Commission urged Congress to pass legislation making it a Federal crime to assassinate the President or Vice President.

Efforts were made to pass such a law on several previous occasions in American history. In 1902, after the assassination of McKinley, bills making it a Federal crime to murder a President passed both houses of Congress, but they died when the Senate refused to accept a compromise measure drawn up by a Congressional conference committee. In 1965 the law finally passed.

Enactment of such a bill will have two important results. First, it will give Federal agencies the power to investigate assassinations and attempted assassinations. As the Warren Commission noted, "at present, Federal agencies participate only upon the sufferance of the local authorities."

The value of this provision is evident to anyone who recalls the performance by Dallas authorities during the two days following the assassination of Kennedy. In an obvious attempt to try the case on television, they held periodic news conferences at which the latest bit of evidence against Oswald was unveiled to the world.

The grotesque climax came when the DA's office announced that it had obtained clinching proof of Oswald's guilt—a map found in Oswald's room which contained a plan for the assassination.

This map, the authorities admitted later, was nothing more sinister than a guide to help Oswald in his job hunting.

The second provision of the Federal assassination bill will make a suspect arrested in connection with an assassination a Federal prisoner. As the Warren Commission noted somewhat wistfully, this will provide the suspect with "Federal protection from vigilante justice and other threats."

The most extreme recommendations for improving the protection of the President came from J. Edgar Hoover.

He agreed with the Warren Commission that "absolute security is neither practical nor possible," explaining that "an approach to complete security would require the President to operate in a sort of vacuum, isolated from the general public and behind impregnable barriers. His travel would be in secret; his public appearances would be behind bulletproof glass."

Hoover nevertheless suggested that several drastic steps be taken.

He proposed that the President drive in an armored car covered with bulletproof glass and kept closed at all times. He recommended the imposition of rigid controls on the President's movements—no walking in public, no mingling with crowds, and the use of television to supplant public appearances whenever possible. He called for close screening of audiences attending Presidential functions, including the use of detecting devices to check for weapons in the crowd. He suggested that when the President must speak in public, he stand behind a bulletproof shield covering the entire rostrum.

The Commission rejected most of these proposals. "Exposure of the President to public view through travel among the people of this country is a great and historic tradition of American life," the Commission said. "Desired by both the President and the public, it is an indispensable means of communication between the two. More often than not, Presidential journeys have served more than one purpose at the same time: ceremonial, administrative, political."

The Commission added: "If the goal were to protect the life of the President, it could be accomplished with reasonable assurance despite the multiple roles he must play. But his very position as representative of the people prevents him from effectively shielding himself from the people. He cannot and will not take the precautions of a dictator or a sovereign.

"Under our system, measures must be sought to afford security without impeding the President's performance of his many functions. The protection of the President must be thorough but inconspicuous to avoid even the suggestion of a garrison state."

Some improvements already have been made in the protective covering provided for the President. The staff of the Protective Research Section, which can play such a vital role in preventing assassination, has been enlarged and improved. Non-governmental consulting firms, like the Rand Corporation and IBM, have been put to work on methods of improving protective techniques. Psychiatrists have provided the Secret Service and the FBI with personality information that would help identify a potential assassin.

In addition, in an effort to avoid the dangerous collapse of communication that permitted Oswald to go unnoticed by the Secret Service, the FBI has been ordered to transmit to the Secret Service all its information on defectors and "subversives, ultrarightists, racists and fascists (a) possessing emotional instability or irrational behavior, (b) who have made threats of bodily harm against officials or employees of Federal, state or local government or officials of a foreign government, (c) who express or have expressed strong or violent anti-U.S. sentiments and who have been involved in bombing or bomb-making or whose past conduct indicates tendencies toward violence, and (d) whose prior acts or statements depict propensity for violence and hatred against organized government."

As a result of this new order, the Secret Service was given thousands of names of persons listed in the FBI files but not previously reported to the Secret Service.

The wording of the new order prompted some understandable concern by at least one member of the Commission, John J. McCloy.

"You have got a pretty broad classification here," McCloy told Alan H. Belmont, the deputy of the FBI. "That may include a good many people in the United States and maybe some members of this Commission."

McCloy added hastily that "I am speaking for myself. There is irrational behavior that I have been guilty of many times. This doesn't mean you are going to send everybody over there, but the names that—all those under your classification, all of those in your opinion come under that classification unless you feel they have some, there is some reason behind it. In other words, you are selective in this list."

Belmont assured McCloy that "we endeavor to use good judgment, sir."

As comprehensive as the new order may be, it is still not clear whether Oswald's name would have been transmitted to the Secret Service under it.

Representative Gerald Ford, another member of the Commission, asked Belmont about this.

Belmont explained that the FBI was now giving the Secret Service the names of all defectors who return to this country. But he was uncertain about whether Oswald's name would have been submitted to the Secret Service under any of the other criteria of the directive. That, Belmont said, was "a question of judgment."

During the Warren Commission's questioning of FBI and Secret Service officials, it became evident that these agencies have concerned themselves almost entirely with overt threats against the President.

Only if a man writes a letter or makes a phone call threatening the President's life will the FBI and the Secret Service become alarmed. Most of the preventive efforts are directed toward the surveillance of those who have made overt threats. This is astonishingly naive. People who write threatening letters or make threatening phone calls are almost certainly mentally disturbed. It is important to keep them under scrutiny. But there is an even more dangerous group—those who plot the assassination of the President covertly. Such persons are likely to act not out of irrational motives, but for political reasons. And they certainly are unlikely to tip their hands in advance.

Even under the new order prepared by the FBI, the agency's eyes remain all but closed to the possibility of cool, calculated political assassination. As the Warren Commission pointed out, under the new criteria, "whether the case should be referred to the Secret Service depends on the existence of a previous history of mental instability, propensity toward violent action, or some similar characteristic, coupled with some evaluation of the capability of the individual or group to further the intention to satisfy a grievance by unlawful means.

"While these tentative criteria are a step in the right direction, they seem unduly restrictive in continuing to require some manifestion of animous against a government official. It is questionable whether such criteria would have resulted in the referral of Oswald to the Secret Service."

The Warren Commission concludes its examination of Presidential protection by declaring that it "can recommend no procedures for the future protection of our Presidents which will guarantee security."

No one can. The best we can hope for are some improvements in the techniques of guarding the President, and even more important, more efficient implementation of the prevailing methods of protection.

We can hope for avoidance of the FBI–Secret Service failures that left Oswald unnoticed by those who might have prevented him from killing. We can hope that buildings will be checked to prevent ambushes like the one staged in Dallas. We can hope for a more realistic recognition of the threat posed not only by the deranged but also by the politically motivated potential assassin. We can hope that every possible preventive precaution will be taken.

But we cannot hope that assassination will be prevented in the future. There are always Oswalds among us. If the odds are any guide, they will strike again.

End

Afterword

Almost three years have passed since the death of President Kennedy, and already the pendulum of history has begun to swing.

In the beginning, during the first months after the Warren Commission issued its Report, there was only silence. Few responsible publications were willing to enunciate in public the widespread doubts about the Report that were constantly being expressed in private. Through the weight of its prestige, and with the assistance of a duly impressed establishment-press, the Warren Commission seemed to have accomplished one of its prime objectives: to still the ugly rumors that followed the assassination, and to exert a calming and re-assuring effect on the nation's thinking about the assassination.

But the political tranquilizer prescribed for the nation by the Warren Commission wore off with surprising speed. Responsible writers and courageous publishers joined to bring temperate, logical analyses of the Warren Report to the public. A body of work emerged—and is emerging still—that points up the weaknesses of the Warren Report with persistent clarity, and that casts grave, perhaps even irrefutable doubt on the Commission's tidy theses.

It would not be immodest to point out, as others already have noted, that *The Unanswered Questions About President Kennedy's Assassination* was the first of these books to challenge the findings and conclusions of the Warren Commission.

The reactions to this book were interesting. People were impressed with the disclosures the book contained, not only because of the nature of those disclosures themselves, but because they were made by "a responsible journalist," a writer with "impressive credentials." Everywhere I went across the country, I heard these words used in discussions of the book. Every review written about the book contained these same phrases. People seemed to want desperately to hear their own doubts expressed by someone they trusted more than they trusted themselves.

There were some attacks. A lawyer who had been on the Warren Commission staff said in a speech in Chicago that the book was a disservice to the United States and damaged this country's image abroad. These are stock attacks on anything that disagrees with an official government position, and I was frankly disappointed at the feebleness of the assault. But I replied, suggesting that nothing could damage American prestige more than the Warren Report itself, and that every attempt to discover the truth could only enhance the image of America as a free society in which official history could be challenged in the public forum. I heard no more from any members of the Warren Commission staff.

The attacks were far outweighed by the praise. Gratifyingly, the favorable comments came from people with a wide variety of political attitudes. For example, the *National Review*, an organ of conservatism, ran a highly laudatory review by M. Stanton Evans, editor of the *Indianapolis News;* equally favorable reviews appeared in the *Harvard Law Record*, the newspaper of the Harvard Law School, and on the liberal Pacifica radio stations across the country.

Since the appearance of this book, many others have been published, and with them has come a new wave of newspaper articles, magazine pieces, and book reviews.

Their number alone is impressive, for it indicates an unflagging desire for the truth about the assassination and a persistent discomfort about the version offered by the Warren Commission. But even more significant is the fact that despite the varied backgrounds of the authors and the various approaches they adopt, all of these works—including my own—generally reach the same conclusions: that the Warren Report was hastily drawn and superficial; that the American people as a result were short-changed on their right to a full and comprehensive official explanation of what took place on November 22, 1963, and that, above all, the Report failed to prove its essential thesis that Oswald acted alone.

Recently, the *New York Review of Books* devoted a cover piece to the assassination. Although purporting to be a review of two new books on the assassination, the piece was a vehicle for writer Richard Popkin to develop his fascinating theory that there were in fact two Oswalds—the real one and a poseur who used Oswald's name and identity to create a trail of confusion before the assassination.

And now, I am told, *The New York Times*, which originally examined the Warren Report closely and found it to be entirely satisfactory, has had second thoughts and has undertaken a new study of the Report in the light of all that has been published which casts doubt both on the Report's adequacy and on *The New York Times'* initial judgment.

Most significant, perhaps, is the call by Richard Goodwin, a former Kennedy aide and speech writer, for a whole new look at the assassination by an independent, non-governmental commission of distinguished and disinterested citizens.

These are amazing developments in so short a time. When *The Unanswered Questions* was written, it was unpopular even to question the findings of the Warren Report. After all, hadn't *The New York Times* and other influential and responsible publications given the Report a favorable reception? It has now grown fashionable not only to question the Report's findings but to suggest—as *The Unanswered Questions* did—that many of them are dead wrong.

But where does all this leave us? Is the whole thing to become a sort of intellectual game called "Catch the Warren Commission?" There is now plenty of material suggesting quite persuasively that the Commission's explanation was less than complete, but where is the public outcry for corrective action? Except for Mr. Goodwin's appeal, there has been none. It is all strangely without passion, as if the public were still unwilling to go all the way and demand official action.

As long as that demand remains unvoiced, there will be no action, no matter how many books are written or how persuasively they demonstrate the flaws in the Warren Report.

One of the striking aspects of the past year or two has been the official silence that greets the arrival of each new book, each new article, each new devastation of the Report. Except for that one speech by a Commission lawyer in Chicago, there was absolutely no response from any official quarter to the appearance of *The Unanswered Questions*. Subsequent books and articles have been greeted with the same inviolate silence.

This is because the Warren Commission, of course, does not exist any longer. It was dissolved as an official agency of the United States Government upon issuance of the Report. Its members have scattered to their respective public and private endeavors: J. Lee Rankin, the Commission's chief counsel, is now Corporation Counsel of the City of New York;

Arlen Spector, another leading member of the Commission's legal staff, is now district attorney of Philadelphia. Other members of the Commission staff hold similarly august posts, and the members of the Commission itself have returned to their government jobs.

Because of its dissolution, the Commission is relieved of the necessity of defending itself in any respect. A commission that does not exist obviously need not answer questions or defend any of its positions. No one, it seems, can be held accountable for the work the Commission did.

So while much important research is being done by private individuals, there is no sign yet of anything being done on an official level to revise or correct the weaknesses of the Report.

We have then come a long way since *The Unanswered Questions* was written. We have, as a nation, been exposed again and again to the proof that the Warren Report fails in its fundamental responsibility to provide the American people with the truth about the assassination. But we have not yet come far enough. We are not yet prepared to take some positive action toward weighing—officially or with official sanction and cooperation—the challenges against the assertions and producing a new and better explanation of how John Kennedy died and why.

Goodwin's proposal—which got only limited attention in the press—or something similar to it, seems to be the answer. What is needed is an independent body of distinguished men —a historian, a psychiatrist, a jurist, a criminologist, a political scientist—who would be given full access to all existing evidence, be assured of full official cooperation, and be given the time, money and investigative resources to begin afresh.

Such a new investigation won't take place until the American people insist that it take place. And time is running out. As the years pass, witnesses die, or their memories grow unreliable, and evidence tends to become blurred by time.

If something is to be done to correct the tragic errors of the Warren Report and to reveal the truth about the assassination —as unpleasant as that truth may be—it must be done soon.

In the foreword to the first edition of this book, I wrote that the examination of the Commission's findings was "a frightening task . . . but an important one which I hope many others will undertake." I added: "If this book casts some rays of light in their path, my first objective will have been attained."

At the time it was written, that was little more than an idle hope. Events have shown, however, that the hope has been more than realized. Many others did indeed undertake the "frightening task;" others are still delving into the Commission's massive product. The writers, scholars and journalists are doing their jobs, finally. It is now up to the public and its representatives to do theirs.

S. F.

New York City
Aug. 1, 1966

Appendix

CHAPTER 1

Page 15

1—It is interesting to recall that Wesley Frazier was, so far as anyone knows, the last person to talk to Oswald before the assassination. Frazier's account of his encounter with Oswald on Nov. 21, of his trip with Oswald from the Book Depository to Irving that evening, and of their return trip to the Depository the next morning, is found in volume II, page 210, and volume VII, page 531, of the Proceedings of the President's Commission on the Assassination of President Kennedy. For purposes of simplification, these proceedings will be identified in these notes as the Proceedings. The Report of the President's Commission on the Assassination of President Kennedy will be referred to in these notes as the Report.

Page 16

2—Patrolman Marrion Baker's testimony is found in volume IV page 248 of the Proceedings. Roy Truly's account is found in Volume III, page 212, and in volume VII pages 380 and 591. The testimony of Howard L. Brennan is in volume III, pages 140, 184, and 211, and in volume XI page 206 of the Proceedings.

Brennan's testimony has become an especial cause of concern to critics of the Report.

Presumably, his observations, and his alone, provided the police at the scene of the assassination with a rough description of the alleged assassin. Yet Brennan admitted to the Commission that his view of the man he saw in the window of the Book Depository was less than ideal.

Brennan tells how he sat across the street from the Book Depository as the President's motorcade approached. Looking over at the building, he said, "I observed quite a few people in different windows. In particular, I saw this one man on the sixth floor which left the window to my knowledge a couple of times. . . ." Brennan

218

says he looked back at the window after he heard the sound of shots "and this man that I saw previous was aiming for his last shot. . . . It appeared to me he was standing up and resting against the left window sill, with gun shouldered to his right shoulder, holding the gun with his left hand and taking positive aim and fired his last shot. . . . He drew the gun back from the window as though he was drawing it back to his side and maybe paused for another second as though to assure hisself (sic) that he hit his mark, and then he disappeared. And at that same moment, I was diving off of that firewall and to the right for bullet protection of this stone wall. . . ."

Asked to describe the man he saw in the window, Brennan replied: "To my best description, a man in his early thirties, fair complexion, slender but neat, neat slender, possibly 5-foot 10 . . . from 160 to 170 pounds."

Page 17

3—The Tippit murder is described on pages 156-176 of the Report, and is detailed in the testimony of the many witnesses to the shooting and to Oswald's subsequent flight.

Page 20

4—Nizer's views are set forth in the preface to an edition of the Report published by Doubleday & Co. "There will be some who will resist persuasion," he says. "The word prejudice derives from the Latin pre judicare—to judge before one has the facts. Those who have so judged before they read the report may not wish their judgments interfered with by fact. They will persist in theories which exploit rumors and inconsistent statements made in the early turmoil. No one is as blind as he who will not see, and sight can be blocked by neurotic adherence to a conviction in which one has and investment of pride or a more sordid interest. We may expect, therefore, that those who cannot be dented by information will continue to carp and propagandize. They will insist that the failure to explain everything perfectly taints all that is explained. They will put the minor factors of the unknown or unknowable against major revelations. They will not joust fairly, by offering facts to be tested against facts, but will utilize a question or a doubt as if it were equivalent to disproof.

"In this sense the report will not end all speculation. But in the historic sense, now that all the facts available have been quarried and justly evaluated, the report will dispose convincingly of the major questions.

"This is the incalculable service rendered by the Commission. This is its achievement in effectuating domestic tranquility and overcoming foreign skepticism. This is its contribution to history."

Page 20

5—The list of leaders of the British committee is an impressive one. Bertrand Russell is a world famous philosopher who has never shunned controversy or unpopular causes. Hugh Trevor-Roper is acknowledged to be one of the world's leading contemporary historians. The committee's efforts, thus far, however, have shown few results. There is another similar committee in Denmark.

CHAPTER 2

Page 26

1—Dr. Hartog's testimony is found in volume VIII page 214 of the Proceedings.

Page 27

2—Oswald's interest in Marxism is described by several persons who knew him as a boy (see pages 383-384 of the Report), and is further supported by a letter he wrote to the Socialist Party in New York when he was 16 (see page 681 of the Report). One of Oswald's friends, Palmer McBride, told the Commission Oswald had suggested joining the Communist Party and had expressed a desire to kill President Eisenhower.

Page 28

3—See pages 668-669 of the Report.

Page 29

4—See page 180 of the Report: "Oswald was questioned intermittently for approximately 12 hours between 2:30 p.m. on Nov. 22 and 11 a.m. on Nov. 24. Throughout this interrogation he denied that he had anything to do either with the assassination of President Kennedy or the murder of Patrolman Tippit."

Page 31

5—Marina Oswald described how Oswald planned the attack on Gen. Walker in her testimony to the Warren Commission. The testimony is included in volumes I, V, and XI of the Proceedings. The report also declares that "In her testimony before the Commission in February 1964, Marina Oswald stated that when Oswald returned home on the night of the Walker shooting, he told her that he had been planning the attempt for two months."

Page 33

6—The suggestion that Oswald might have been in the employ of the CIA or the FBI necessarily must remain entirely conjectural. It is no secret that these agencies rely heavily on paid informants and tipsters, often drawn from the ranks of the underworld or from subversive organizations. Neither the FBI nor the CIA is likely, however, ever to admit that Oswald was such an informant, since this would raise a flood of questions about the morality and ethics of the system utilized by these agencies.

Page 34

7—See page 407 of the Report: "Following his arrest, he was interviewed by the police, and at his own request, by an agent of the FBI."

Page 34

8—This comment is supported by the biography of Jack Ruby contained in the Report (Appendix XVI).

CHAPTER 3

Page 41

1—See page 180 of the Report: "Captain Fritz of the homicide and robbery bureau did most of the questioning, but he kept no notes and there were no stenographic or tape recordings."

Page 47

2—The testimony of Mrs. Earlene Roberts is contained in volume VI page 434 and volume VII page 439 of the Proceedings.

Page 49

3—See page 206 of the Report: "Police officers on the third floor testified that they carefully checked all persons for credentials, and most newsmen indicated that after Batchelor imposed security they were required to identify themselves by their press cards. Special Agent Sorrels of the Secret Service stated that he was requested to present credentials on some of his visits to the third floor."

Page 50

4—See page 209 of the Report: "During the night, between 2:30 and 3 a.m., the local office of the FBI and the sheriff's office received telephone calls from an unidentified man who warned that a committee had decided 'to kill the man that killed the President.' Shortly after, an FBI agent notified the Dallas police of the anonymous threat. The police department and ultimately Chief Curry were informed of both threats."

Page 52

5—See page 342 of the Report: "In answer to one question, Wade said that Oswald belonged to the 'Free Cuba Committee.' A few reporters spoke up correcting Wade and among the voices was that of Jack Ruby." Ruby himself tells of correcting Wade. His testimony is found in volume V page 181 and volume XIV page 504.

CHAPTER 4

Page 56

1—See Dwight Macdonald's critique of the Warren Report in the March 1965 issue of Esquire.

CHAPTER 5

Page 95

1—See Mrs. Hill's testimony in volume VI page 205 of the Proceedings.

CHAPTER 6

Page 109

1—Mrs. Clemmons was interviewed by George and Patricia Nash and she is quoted by them in an article that appeared in the New Leader of Oct. 12, 1964.

CHAPTER 7

Page 128

1—See Kenneth O'Donnell's testimony, volume VII page 440 of the Proceedings.

CHAPTER 9

Page 159

1—See page 792-793 of the Report: "Before she opened the Singapore in 1947, Eva Grant engaged in the sale of metal products. In that year she met Paul Roland Jones, who allegedly was seeking customers for iron pipe and whom she referred to Hyman Rubenstein. Jones had, at about that time, been convicted of attempting to bribe the newly elected sheriff of Dallas. On Oct. 24, 1947, he was arrested for violating narcotics statutes. . . . During the two years in which Jones was appealing his conviction (NB— It is not clear here whether the reference is to Jones' conviction for attempted bribery or his conviction for a narcotics violation which, as we shall see in a moment, also is on the record according to the Report.) he and other criminals frequented the Singapore Club, then operated by Jack Ruby.

"Intensive investigation to determine whether Jack Ruby was criminally or otherwise connected with Jones' narcotics violation leads the commission to conclude Ruby probably was not involved. A search of the files of the Bureau of Narcotics disclosed no record that either Hyman or Jack had been prosecuted by Federal authorities in 1947. Jack, Hyman and Eva denied participating in any narcotics activities. Jones and his co-conspirators also denied that Jack was a participant. One of Jones' confederates reported after the shooting of Oswald that although Jones 'propositioned' the two brothers concerning narcotics, they refused to participate. Moreover, when one of the conspirators was arrested with 48 pounds of raw opium in his possession, he implicated Jones and another person, both of whom were convicted, but he did not implicate Ruby or his brother."

Page 159

2—See page 794 of the Report: "In 1954, Ruby's Vegas asso-
ciate, Joe Bonds, was convicted of sodomy and sent to a Texas
penitentiary to serve an 8-year sentence."

Page 162

3—See page 801 of the Report: ". . . the evidence indicates
that Ruby was keenly interested in policemen and their work . . .
the report of present and past members of the Dallas Police Department as well as Ruby's employees and acquaintances indicate
that Ruby's police friendships were far more widespread than those
of the average citizen."

And further along on that same page: "From the time that
Ruby arrived in Dallas in 1947, he was friendly with numerous
underworld figures."

Page 164

4—The Report (page 346) identifies this witness as Garnett C.
Hallmark, general manager of the Nichols Parking Garage, which
is adjacent to the Carousel Club. Hallmark's testimony is found in
volume XV page 488 of the Proceedings.

Page 168

5—Sgt. Patrick T. Dean made these statements to the Warren
Commission. His testimony is found in volume V page 254 and
volume XII page 415. The account provided here is taken directly
from the testimony.

CHAPTER 10

Page 174

1—This incident is described in the Report on page 673. It is
based on testimony offered by Marguerite Oswald herself. Her
testimony is contained in volume I page 126 of the Proceedings.

CHAPTER 12

Page 209

1—See page 461 of the Report: "The Secret Service has embarked upon a complete overhaul of its research activities. The
staff of the Protective Research Section (PRS) has been aug-
mented, and a Secret Service inspector has been put in charge of
this operation. With the assistance of the President's Office of
Science and Technology, and of the Advanced Research Projects
Agency of the Department of Defense, it has obtained the services
of outside consultants, such as the Rand Corp., International Business Machines Corp., and a panel of psychiatric and psychological

experts. It has received assistance also from data processing experts at the CIA and from a specialist in psychiatric prognostication at Walter Reed Hospital."

Bibliography

In preparing this book, I naturally read everything that was available dealing with the assassination of President Kennedy. Some material came across my desk in the normal course of my work as a newspaperman. Some came to me unpublished from other sources. Still more was elicited through conversations with persons knowledgeable about special aspects of the assassination. It is therefore impossible to offer a comprehensive list of sources for this book. Here, however, is a bibliography of a few basic items that are bound to be of interest to anyone desirous of examining the Warren Report critically.

BUCHANAN, Thomas G. *Who Killed Kennedy?* New York: Putnam, 1964.

FORD, Gerald. *Portrait of the Assassin.* New York: Simon & Schuster, 1965.

JOESTEN. Joachim. *Oswald: Assassin or Fall Guy?* New York: Marzani & Munsell, 1964.

MACDONALD, Dwight. *A Critique of the Warren Report.* New York: Esquire (magazine), March 1965.

NASH, George and Patricia et al. *Critical Reactions to the Warren Report.* New York: Marzani & Munsell, 1964.

SALANDRIA, Vincent J. *The Warren Report.* New York: Liberation (magazine) March 1965.

SMITH, Merriman et al. *Four Days.* New York: United Press International and American Heritage, 1964.

WARREN, Earl et al. *Proceedings of the President's Commission on the Assassination of President Kennedy.* Vol. I-XXVI. Washington: U. S. Govt. Printing Office, 1964.

WARREN, Earl et al. *Report of the President's Commission on the Assassination of President Kennedy.* Washington: U. S. Govt. Printing Office, 1964.

Page 210
2—The order was issued to the FBI by its director, J. Edgar Hoover, and by Alan H. Belmont, the assistant to the director of the FBI, on Dec. 26, 1963, just a month after Kennedy's assassination. Belmont discusses the order in his testimony, which is found in volume V page 1 of the Proceedings.